So You're Going to Run a Library

So You're Going to Run a Library
A Library Management Primer

Dave Sutton

1995
LIBRARIES UNLIMITED, INC.
Englewood, Colorado

LIBRARIES UNLIMITED, INC.
P.O. Box 6633
Englewood, CO 80155-6633
1-800-237-6124

Library of Congress Cataloging-in-Publication Data

Sutton, Dave.
    So you're going to run a library : a library management primer /
Dave Sutton.
    xvi, 190 p. 17x25 cm.
    Includes bibliographical references and index.
    ISBN 1-56308-306-X
    1. Library administration.   I. Title.
Z678.S89   1995
025.1--dc20   95-4443
                                                                   CIP

This book is dedicated to Trish, who may have to show someone else how to use it or use it herself, if her children, my granddaughters, are going to have libraries in their schools.

CONTENTS

PREFACE

The author of this volume has worked with volunteers who helped establish libraries; with teachers who assumed the role of librarians by getting professional training and on-the-job experience simultaneously; with school librarians sharing their expertise between two or more building programs; as well as full-time library media specialists working with other professional media specialists, staff, student aides, and volunteers.

This book is intended as an introduction for those who wish an opportunity to provide a library with organized information for patrons from children through adults, for those who have been chosen to do so, perhaps by accident more than by considered choice, and for those assigned to the task, reluctant as well as accidental. The volume begins at the beginning, explaining not only how things happen, but why and what procedures are important to follow. It is a "how-to" guide for the beginner, someone who has little if any experience in libraries yet is expected to manage a small library in a school, community, church, or corporation, with little supervision.

This volume could also be used as a training guide for coordinators with responsibility for library programs in schools with paraprofessionals assigned to individual buildings, or for public librarians who must prepare accidental librarians with one or more workshops or training sessions.

No brief introduction can possibly answer all the questions of someone undertaking responsibility for a library. Just as students in a master's program rely on several textbooks and outside readings for their courses, this book cannot stand alone. An extensive annotated bibliography directs readers to additional sources of information. Also, readers are encouraged to ask librarians for help when questions or problems arise.

INTRODUCTION

This book is designed as a primer or guidebook for someone who has little or no experience working in a library and suddenly must do so: an accidental opportunity in a school, community, church, or corporation. You may have volunteered, been chosen or drafted, or been reassigned to manage a library, with or without premeditation and usually without formal preparation. Several scenarios may illustrate the creation of an accidental library manager.

THE VOLUNTEER

A conversation heard at a meeting of parents, a church bazaar, or a bridge club might be, "Our school (or church or town) needs a library. No one else seems to have thought of this. Perhaps we three should set up a library for children (or a congregation or neighbors)." "We three" may be reduced to you as your fellow workers acknowledge other commitments.

THE DRAFTEE

"Someone has to figure out how to store these government reports so we can use them when we need to refer to them. Because you have asked us to order more documents than anyone else, you are the logical person to organize and retrieve them." Interest in or need for information is not always an indicator of eagerness to file and find again. Further, your interest may be in a narrow part of the subject, and other documents may have a much wider audience.

REASSIGNMENT

Changes in curriculum, lack of interest in a subject area for whatever reason, or a reduction in school population or school budget support can reduce the number of teachers or other personnel in any school. Budget cuts in an organization usually reduce staff, because personnel costs are heavy. "Personnel changes in our agency for next year mean we must shift your position. I'd like to suggest that you consider undertaking responsibility for our library (or media center or information agency)." Though such a statement at first may appear to be a request, it may be an assignment rather than an option.

DO YOU REALLY WANT TO DO THIS?

Before approaching any principal, minister, mayor, or other official to volunteer to organize a library, or before accepting the challenge of the administrator making a reassignment to the library, it is important to ask some basic questions so you can begin to understand the ground rules. Few persons who have not worked in a library have a clear picture of what actually goes on there. What can be viewed at a glance will be patrons using the library, questions being answered, materials and equipment being used in the library, and items being checked out for use outside the library. Not so easily observed are those activities that keep the library running smoothly.

Activities that must be understood so they can be implemented include work involved in choosing new materials and equipment for the library. Precise steps must be followed for ordering, receiving, and preparing new items so they can be shelved in their proper location. Some procedures must be maintained to insure consistency in placing items correctly on shelves, where they can be easily found by patrons. A standard process for doing so is essential. Maintaining a record of who has what items is necessary if library materials are going to be taken and returned. In some situations, library users must be taught how to use the library, how to find items on shelves, and how to use the references they have identified once they are located. These are major tasks, but by no means all that must be considered. Anyone embarking on library management needs to understand expectations of administrators and perhaps a little of what these persons to whom you will be responsible understand about managing a library.

ASK BEFORE YOU LEAP

Responses to the following six questions may help you decide if this move is a good or not-so-good endeavor, whether the assignment is a problem or an opportunity, and whether the responsibility for patrons, collection, services, and facility involves tasks that would be interesting to undertake.

1. How much time will you be allocated to devote to the management of the program? Full-time or part-time?

2. If part-time, who will be in the library if you are not there?

Some school districts assign a teacher to the school library for part of the day, and the remainder of the time is spent teaching a subject area. Or, a teacher-librarian might be assigned to more than one building. Accepting an appointment to run a library would be challenging enough, without having additional responsibilities for an academic subject or for a second building.

If the assignment is only part-time, will you have clerical assistance, either part-time or full-time? When a clerk has a full-time assignment to a library and the librarian is only part-time, the clerk will probably be perceived as the one in charge. Part-time persons, even though responsible for management, will have difficulty when the librarian is away much of the time. Even less desirable is relying on volunteers when you are in another location.

It is difficult to manage any library with volunteers as the only additional support, particularly a public library. You may be unable to leave the building for any time, even lunch or dinner, if you are the only person in the library. Volunteers in a community are often volunteers for more than one activity, and they may not always make the library their highest priority. Volunteers also must respond to family needs before fulfilling an outside commitment.

In the corporate setting, dividing time between an information center and any other assignment may cause problems when both situations demand immediate attention. Also, if your primary interest is in the practical application of information to projects of personal interest, interruption to secure information for others may cause you tension and stress.

3.   What professional assistance would be available when you have questions? The district coordinator of school libraries? School librarian in another building? Outside consultant? Someone in another corporate library? State library consultant?

It is important to know who can be called for assistance with problems related to management and materials selection, for answering reference questions that require information not readily located, and for many other needs.

Throughout this volume it is suggested that going beyond the procedures outlined would require professional assistance. Whom can you ask? When an activity does not seem to be working—a procedure is unclear or an expectation is not being met—having an expert to call on would take some of the uncertainty out of the appointment. Such a consultant must be readily available through communication links or one-on-one interviews.

4.   How will you know when you are doing well, i.e., what is considered an adequate, good, better, or best library program?

5.   Is the administrator interested in the program being adequate, good, better, or best?

Although it may be easier to work for administrators with low expectations for an information center, it is difficult to get such administrators to allocate funds for what they consider a low-priority program. Further, these administrators, not knowing what is involved in the management of an information center, may expect a smoothly running operation in inadequate space, with a collection that requires much updating, and activities that cannot be accomplished by a single person working part-time.

Library users will also have expectations. Information about anticipated patron usage of the information center is necessary before undertaking the assignment. Assurances are needed that the information center will be able to meet their basic needs.

6.   What will the budget be and who controls expenditures?

What seems at first to be a large sum of money quickly shrinks when the apprentice librarian begins to analyze how funds are spent. In information centers where the budget includes personnel, this figure is usually a large proportion of the budget. Second, money must be provided for purchase of new materials and equipment for the collection. Magazine subscriptions must be renewed, new books and audiovisual materials ordered, and equipment repaired and replaced. Supplies to process new materials, send letters, and create bulletin boards are also necessary. If you are to improve your skills, a travel budget must be available for workshops and conferences.

Today, much information is obtained from outside sources, using communication links for online databases and telefacsimile (fax) transmission. Interlibrary loan may require mailing costs or other forms of delivery. Communication links, telephone lines, fax machines, E-mail capability, and online public access catalogs, among other sources, have their costs included in the budget, and such costs are continuing rather than one-time purchases. Sufficient funds in all areas are necessary for programs to be useful and effective.

You should know the amount budgeted for the library and be able to issue purchase orders or other authorizations to purchase items, receive shipments, and confirm receipt for payments. When an order must be approved by one or more administrators, delays may seriously hinder timely collection development, equipment repair, or purchase of necessary supplies.

When all the questions posed here as well as any others you may have are answered, and the assignment has been accepted, you may want an introduction to the dimensions of the task. This book identifies the basic activities and explains how to begin to manage an information center or library. Simple theory is provided to explain the reasons for doing the tasks as outlined. Alternate actions are suggested to accomplish a task, or you may review theory to help outline steps to follow to the final outcome or product.

Suggested references are given in the annotated bibliography at the end of this book. These sources can expand your knowledge about the management of libraries and information centers.

Library and information science professionals, like members of other professions, have their own terminology. Many of these terms are defined in detail where they are used in the text; others are given longer definitions in the glossary at the ends of some chapters. Terms that are further defined are shown in italics the first time they are used.

The format is to discuss decisions you must make and actions you may take. Not all actions will generate the reaction you anticipate. In case this happens, alternative actions may be proposed. Decisions, actions, and alternative actions are called out to the reader with special headings.

ASK A LIBRARIAN

Explanations are presented at a basic level. At a more expanded level of performance, additional information may be required beyond what can be provided in this volume. An icon (📖) indicates it's time for you to **Ask a Librarian**.

You may want to consult the annotated bibliography for answers in the literature. Or you may turn to a nearby school or special librarian or to the nearest public library for advice that will make it possible to continue building an effective library program. When the challenge is an offer you cannot refuse, you will accept the opportunity. This book can be a starting point to help you begin.

Chapter 1

YOUR LIBRARY

Working in a library is one of the most interesting opportunities available for helping others. Providing information when it is needed is personally rewarding. You will have the opportunity to make a contribution to the lives of members of your community, whether a school, a public library, or a special library. This chapter will explain some of the management tasks you will be expected to perform and clarify why library collections are so carefully organized.

BEGIN AT THE BEGINNING

Open the door of your library and walk into your new world. What will be expected of you? At best, only 50 percent of the management of any library, media center, or information center is immediately obvious to casual observers. Most people, when asked what library staff members do, would reply, "Check books in and out of the library." Shelving books, buying new books, keeping order in the library, and collecting fines round out their perception of the array of tasks. Behind the scenes, a wide variety of management and clerical tasks must be done to keep an operation running smoothly, and this means that decisions are carefully considered. After you decide what to do and how to do it, you must see that your decisions are implemented with consistency. A pattern of steps is recorded and further activities are repeated accurately. Any changes in established procedures are recorded in your procedures manual.

THE PROCEDURES MANUAL

A helpful means to achieve consistency in actions is to record procedures, perhaps in a loose-leaf notebook. If you move into a facility with an existing manual, then the various policies and procedures to be followed in managing the library are available. Compare this manual with the sample table of contents below. Procedures missing from the manual that you think you will need can be outlined, tested, revised, and added to the manual.

ACTION ONE: Check existing manual.

Check your manual against the table of contents below. When an item is missing, begin to locate the information and add what you discover. The manual provides a base for decision making and a means of recording deviations to established policies and procedures or adding missing items.

Table of Contents

    I. Calendar for the Year (including information about required reports, ordering dates, etc.)

  II. Staff
- A. Other librarians in the immediate area or system (all types)
- B. Users, i.e., teachers and students in the school, residents of the service area, clients in the corporation, the library board, and others
- C. Important telephone numbers, i.e., business managers, other libraries in the area

  III. Philosophy of Services

  IV. Schedules
- A. Master schedule for the school, year-long schedule for the corporation or public library
- B. Method of scheduling class visits for students or hours of operation for other agencies
- C. Other information related to scheduled times

  V. Blueprint of the Library
- A. Floor plan
- B. Hours of operation
- C. Rules for patron use of facility
  1. Behavior in, or instructions for coming to the library for schools
  2. Instructions concerning database use

  VI. Circulation Procedures
- A. Books and audiovisual media
- B. Reserve and reference materials
- C. Equipment
- D. Interlibrary loan regulations and processes

  VII. Acquisitions and Budget
- A. Selection policy (includes what to do in case of complaint for school and public libraries)
- B. Purchasing procedures (including sample forms, how to order, when to order, where to order)
- C. Budget information
- D. Processing information (including how to place the library's holdings on any union list)
- E. Billing information for online database use

  VIII. Inventory Information
- A. Maintenance of equipment
- B. Weeding procedures

IX. Central Services
   A. Responsibilities to any central agency
   B. What's available from any central agency and how to order
   C. Delivery of materials to and from a central agency

X. Information for a Substitute Librarian

XI. Guidelines for In-Service Training
   A. Staff of the media center
   B. Faculty of the school or users of the public or corporation library
   C. Students in the school (including sequence of library skills training)

XII. Local, State, National Standards, or Corporate and Agency Requirements

XIII. Helpful Hints

XIV. Glossary of Terms

XV. Appendix
   A. Five-year management plan
   B. Manual for volunteers
   C. Manual for users (includes services offered and may be divided by type of user such as student or faculty, corporate manager or corporate chemist)
   D. Manual for paid assistants or student helpers
   E. Manual for staff (includes job descriptions and an organization chart of the library)
   F. Supplier catalogs (unless a separate file is maintained)

ALTERNATIVE ACTION ONE: Create a manual.

When no manual is available, the sample table of contents can be used to collect information about library operations so that they are planned, executed, and evaluated for success. As suggested earlier, a loose-leaf notebook allows you to add information easily. The author has also punched holes in pocket portfolios so that they can be added to a notebook to hold examples such as bookmarks or bibliographies that you do not want to punch for the notebook.

Any changes in policies or procedures are to be recorded in this manual. Following the procedures manual should help maintain consistency over time.

The manual will identify and describe activities involved in day-to-day management. It outlines specific activities needed for information to flow to and from users. Areas where management concepts are given numerical identifiers, such as hours of operation (e.g., 9:00 A.M. to 5:00 P.M.) and circulation policy (e.g., two weeks for books, one day for videotapes), are both written in the policy manual and posted for patrons.

When the library is a new addition to any agency, decisions must be made, information gathered, and procedures established in each of these categories. Categories will be expanded throughout the remainder of this volume, although not in the order shown here. Although many topics to be included in a procedures manual will be addressed in more depth throughout the book, not all will be. That is, patron use of any library is discussed in this book, although actual rules governing use will be determined by you and your administrators, and those specific rules recorded in your procedures manual.

Management as a process is not discussed in depth. Several books about management tasks such as planning are listed in the annotated bibliography. This bibliography also suggests sources for forms that might be needed in managing a library. If you wish to purchase supplies or forms from a commercial vendor, write to the following vendors for supply catalogs:

Bro-Dart	Demco	Gaylord
500 Arch St.	P.O. Box 621	P.O. Box 4901
Williamsport, PA 17705	Valley Forge, PA 19481	Syracuse, NY 13221

The Highsmith Co., Inc.
W5527 106
P.O. Box 800
Ft. Atkinson, WI 53528-0800

FINDING THINGS IN THE LIBRARY

Once you have reviewed any existing manual or begun creating a new procedures manual, you should determine the system used to place materials on shelves. One of the differences between a library and a less well-organized collection of materials is that library materials have been identified in such a way that anyone who wishes to use the contents of any item will be able to locate it and use the information in it.

Although other organization patterns exist, two systems will be discussed in this book. These schemes have been carefully designed by librarians, and their designs are modified regularly to accommodate new vocabulary terms as subjects are renamed, descriptors for new information developed, and new formats created in our constantly changing world. Parts of the design include *classification* (where the materials fit into an established scheme for the organization of knowledge and indicating their "address" or location on the library shelves) and assigning *subject headings* (the word or words used to describe the contents of the materials in the *card catalog* or in the *online public access catalog*).

The final feature is the way information is filed. In a card catalog, these rules are important because they maintain consistency for users. Specific rules may seem less important for online public access catalogs, where searching can be expanded or decreased more easily. Nonetheless, if items are not entered consistently, they must be retrieved through different strategies, and this would confuse both the librarian and the users.

Classification Systems

Materials are analyzed to determine the major topic covered in each item. This topic is then given a code, called a classification number or call number. Books on the same subject will have the same call number. Most libraries in the United States have been organized under one of two major classification schemes: Dewey Decimal Classification (DDC) system or Library of Congress Classification (LCC) system. You might wish to use an alternative system, but developing a means for organizing a body of knowledge is not easy.

DECISION ONE: Identify the library's classification system.

- Dewey: Used by most smaller public libraries and school libraries
- LC: Used by larger public libraries and most academic libraries
- Alternative system: Difficult for the next librarian in the position

ACTION ONE: Use Dewey.

With the Dewey system, all knowledge is divided into 10 classes as follows:

000 General Works (encyclopedias)

100 Philosophy

200 Religion

300 Sociology (also includes folktales and fairy tales in the 398s)

400 Philology/Language (dictionaries and books in foreign languages)

500 Pure Science (theoretical science)

600 Applied Science (putting science to work)

700 Fine Arts (art, music, sports)

800 Literature (however, fiction and picture books are not usually given 800 numbers)

900 History, Biography, Geography

The first part of the call number consists of three numbers. If further division is needed, additional numbers follow a decimal point, or as many numbers as needed to place an item in its exact location in the system. Items with Dewey Decimal Classification system call numbers might look like figure 1.1.

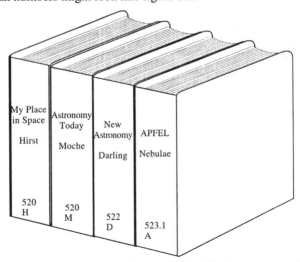

Fig. 1.1. Items with Dewey Decimal Classification system call numbers.

ALTERNATIVE ACTION ONE: Use Library of Congress.

The Library of Congress Classification (LCC) system is made up of letters and numbers. Letters place the material under a broad subject category as follows:

A — General Works, Polygraphy

B, pt. 1, B-BJ — Philosophy

B, pt. 2, BL-BX — Religion

C — Auxiliary Sciences of History

D — General and Old World History

E-F — American History

G — Geography, Anthropology, Folklore, Manners and Customs, Recreation

H — Social Sciences

J — Political Science

KD — Law of the United Kingdom and Ireland

KF — Law of the United States

L — Education

M — Music and Books on Music

N — Fine Arts

P-PA — Philology, Linguistics, Classical Philology, Classical Literature

PB-PH — Modern European Languages

PG, in part — Russian Literature

PJ-PM — Languages and Literature of Asia, Africa, Oceania, America, Mixed Languages, Artificial Languages

PN, PR, PS, PZ — Literature (General), English and American Literature, Fiction in English, Juvenile Literature

PQ, pt. 1 — French Literature

PQ, pt. 2 — Italian, Spanish, and Portuguese Literature

PT, pt. 1 — German Literature

PT, pt. 2 — Dutch and Scandinavian Literatures

Q — Science

R — Medicine

S — Agriculture, Plant and Animal Industry, Fish Culture and Fisheries, Hunting Sports

T — Technology

U — Military Science

V — Naval Science

Z — Bibliography and Library Science

One reason that Library of Congress is usually not chosen for school library media centers or small public libraries is that many books would fall under "PZ" rather than having the more distinct categories available under Dewey. Materials classified by Library of Congress are housed first by the letters of the alphabet and then by the numbers. A shelf with books using Library of Congress numbers would look like figure 1.2:

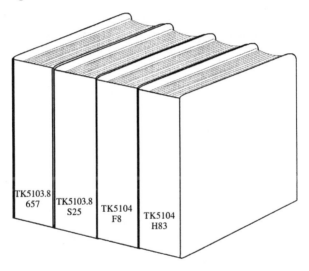

Fig. 1.2. Items with Library of Congress Classification system numbers.

ALTERNATIVE ACTION TWO: Use an alternative system.

It may be that you will be in charge of a collection that is very small, such as in a day care center, and you may prefer to organize books in some alternative system. That is, you may choose to place all books that tell stories about or have facts about animals on one shelf, books on community helpers on another shelf, books on plants on another, and so on. Small collections may be better organized in a way that is logical for users of that collection. However, keep in mind that when you design your own system, you should keep a record of how that system works so that you and any others can follow the system consistently. Few things are as disconcerting as being unable to locate information because you do not understand the method used to classify the materials.

When one classification system has been in place, and all materials have been assigned appropriate subject headings, it is unlikely that you will want to change the system, especially for a library with a large collection. The process of change is called converting records, and if a switch is being made from one system to another, this change is usually a total redoing of what has been done. That is another good reason to use Dewey or LC. It will save someone a great deal of work in the future. Also, commercial companies from whom you buy books can often supply catalog cards with Dewey or LC numbers already printed on the cards.

Some libraries use an accession number system. They number each item as it is entered into the collection and house that item in order by this number. This means the newest item is on the last shelf, and anyone looking for materials on a certain subject will look in many different locations based on when an item was purchased.

Sometimes librarians place books on shelves using a classification scheme and place other formats (e.g., CD-ROM, audiotape) using the accession number system. This is another decision the person organizing a new collection must make.

DECISION TWO: To classify some or all formats?

Formats include, among others

- Books

- Films

- Videotapes

- Filmstrips

- Microfiche

- Toys and games

A single classification system for all formats is simpler to use. Although using accession numbers may simplify the process initially for the librarian, it complicates it for users for the remainder of the life of the item. For example, under the accession number system, someone looking for materials on astronomy would have to find accession numbers 25, 500, 873, and 2001, rather than finding all four items together under Dewey number 520. Furthermore, patrons will have to consult an often out-of-date list to find items rather than just going to a section of shelves where like subjects are located.

Assigning Subject Headings

Materials can be given only one classification or call number. However, many items provide information on more than one topic. Because the item cannot be physically divided, several or many subject headings are assigned to each item, and additional references to the item are found in the card catalog or online catalog.

DECISION THREE: Choose subject headings.

- Sears

- LC

- Alternative such as ERIC

The two most popular references listing subject headings are *Sears List of Subject Headings,* published in its 14th edition in 1991, and *Library of Congress Subject Headings,* which is published annually. These two differ in the number of headings. Sears has over 6,000 subject headings, and Library of Congress has almost 200,000 headings from which to choose. For specialized collections, there are subject heading lists or thesauri that will help, such as ERIC for education terms or *Reader's Guide* for current collections.

For smaller libraries, Sears is the better choice. LC belongs in larger or more specialized collections. If the library is automated, the vendor or a previous librarian who designed the system may have designated LC headings. In this case, cataloging information from a jobber or other bibliographic source will come directly into the computer.

Sometimes "matching the school's curriculum" is given as a reason for choosing alternative headings; however, curriculum changes and educational terminology lack consistency, that is, making a heading for a new education term that may not survive over time, rather than subsuming the subject under a broader term in Sears or LC.

What may be familiar to one set of teachers will be unfamiliar to new teachers as staff and curricula change. It is this author's belief that it is easier over the long term to use a standard subject heading list rather than be prey to short-term idiosyncratic terms generated with curriculum modifications.

The problem with all subject heading lists is they evolve and change over time. Thus the library may have books listed under NEGROES, BLACK AMERICANS, and AFRO-AMERICANS, depending on when the item was cataloged. Keeping any kind of consistency in subject headings is a challenge. As each item is added to the catalog, its subject headings must be checked against both the subject heading list and what is already in the catalog. If there is a difference, then a decision must be made. If a new heading or an updated heading is chosen, the easiest procedure is to put a cross-reference in the catalog such as "NEGROES. See also BLACK AMERICANS," and a second cross-reference that would read "BLACK AMERICANS. See also NEGROES."

Sometimes, however, all the old items are best re-cataloged with the new subject headings, though this is a time-consuming process. This is a decision to be made in each library each time the problem occurs.

Care is taken to make sure a subject heading is assigned only when information on that subject is found in the item. Items assigned incorrect subject headings will be given credit for information on topics not actually covered. When users try to find information in the item, they will be as frustrated as they would be opening what is advertised as a box of chocolates and finding it filled with macaroni.

Arrangement on the Shelves

As stated above, classification systems dictate the call number for each item—the address of the item. This number, and it may be a combination of letters and numbers or numbers with a decimal point, is used to locate items on library shelves. Most call numbers have a second line, which indicates the author's last name. Most libraries use the first three letters of the author's last name as shown in figure 1.3.

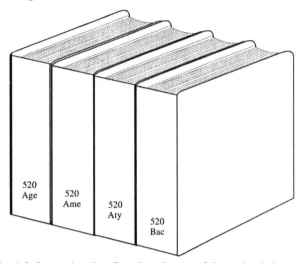

Fig. 1.3. Items showing first three letters of the author's last name.

DECISION FOUR: Do I need Cutter numbers?

For larger library collections, the author's last name is designated using Cutter numbers, a code devised to spell names with letters and numbers. This provides a unique call number for every book on the shelf. Items with Dewey and Cutter numbers would be arranged like figure 1.4. Cutter numbers are created using a Cutter table (available from Libraries Unlimited).

A4L7   B5S6   D503   F74   G89A3   H6H6

Fig. 1.4. Cutter numbers.

If the library has used Cutter numbers in the past, there should be a Cutter table already available.

Most libraries using Dewey separate fiction books from nonfiction and shelve fiction in alphabetical order by the author's last name, rather than in the literature section of the Dewey classification system. An example of a shelf of fiction books would look like figure 1.5.

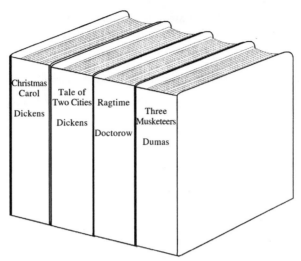

Fig. 1.5. Example of a shelf of fiction books.

Obviously, classification schemes mean little if materials are not kept at their proper address. Materials should be shelved by call number with signs over various sections to help patrons locate the right call number. The shelves will have to be "read," or put back in order, from time to time, depending on the amount of use.

Because users may re-shelve incorrectly, they may be asked to leave any materials taken from the shelf on library tables rather than re-shelving them. That, however, assumes that the library staff is large enough to re-shelve all the used materials. Patrons may have to learn how to re-shelve their own materials. School librarians sometimes give students a bookmark to place on the shelf when they remove an item, so that it can be correctly replaced if they choose not to check it out.

One way for an apprentice librarian to begin to understand what is available in a library is to read the shelves. Check the shelves item by item to confirm that call numbers follow the proper sequence. In the process of removing a mis-shelved item and re-shelving it, you can be introduced to the item, albeit briefly. Shelves should be read frequently to confirm that all re-shelving has been done accurately and that the next user can find materials at their correct addresses.

Reading the shelves and shelving returned materials require a basic under-standing of alphabetical and number order for the classification scheme chosen. Please refer back to the discussion of choice of classification scheme (beginning on page 4) for some examples of proper order.

Ephemeral Information

Important information may be clipped from newspapers and magazines and stored for future use in files kept in boxes or filing cabinets called vertical files. Inexpensive pamphlets and government documents are also sources of current information that does not fit easily on book shelves. Clippings, pamphlets, articles, pictures, and other items provide some of the most up-to-date information on current topics, but they do require time to clip, property stamp, and label with a filing subject heading.

DECISION FIVE: Which subject headings should be used for ephemeral materials?

Again, you may wish to be consistent with subject headings throughout the library.

ACTION ONE: Use identical headings to other items.

A standard subject heading list may be used to label file folders or pamphlets, insuring that ephemeral information storage matches the subject headings for other materials, e.g., Sears or LC.

ALTERNATIVE ACTION ONE: Use an alternative list.

For others, an alternative subject heading list is chosen.

ALTERNATIVE ACTION TWO: Develop your own list.

When you have access to a computer, any subject heading list of information in a special file may be maintained on a database. However, users may have difficulty using alternative headings for information.

Ephemeral files must be kept current. Much of their value is in their immediacy. A date is to be written or stamped on each item as it is placed in the file to help with *weeding* at a later time.

Further information on developing this part of the collection can be found in the books cited in the bibliography (page 171).

To Catalog or Not to Catalog?

You need not be overly concerned about original cataloging, that is, assigning classification numbers or subject headings. Many items come from the book wholesalers or jobbers ready for the shelves, or *preprocessed*. That is, catalog cards, book pockets, and charge cards are provided, and perhaps plastic jackets placed over the book jacket, making the book more attractive to the user and protecting it. Most books published in the United States have the cataloging information on the reverse side of the title page. This is called Cataloging in Publication (CIP) and is prepared by the staff at the Library of Congress. CIP may be used to create cards or records for a retrieval system. In an online cataloging system, most items may be already on the *bibliographic database*. If you have had no experience with cataloging and classifying, and the organization of information is an immediate need, ▢**Ask a Librarian**.

A technical services librarian can clarify the basics of acquiring and organizing a collection; however, cataloging and classification of information, the science of library science, cannot be mastered through brief explanations. Discussion of correct classification and practice in cataloging are needed just to begin to assign addresses and subject headings, and it is only after much experience that one becomes proficient.

Correct classification is critical; when classification is incomplete or incorrect, material will be assigned an incorrect address, placing it in a location away from other materials on that subject. Although this would not be detrimental to the user who finds a call number and locates a single item, it is undesirable for the person who might find more information in the correct location simply because it was there on the shelf. Casual browsers will expect to find all items on a single subject or topic in a single location, or they might find additional items through a serendipitous encounter. More information on preparation of materials for the shelf is given in chapter 7.

Location and Storage of Equipment

Equipment requires special attention when planning for shelving. Most equipment requires tall, deep, and wide bin shelving or extensive floor space for rolling carts that hold equipment. Different machines are different sizes, and standard shelving may not work. For example, you may be responsible for

- 16mm projectors
- Filmstrip projectors
- Overhead projectors
- Videotape recorders
- Videotape players
- Cameras of all types
- Record, tape, and CD players

Each piece of equipment that is used only in the library or in the building should be placed on a rolling cart for ease of access. This means that the storage area must be larger than a closet.

The simplest way to give a call number to equipment is to number the bin and place that number on the piece of equipment. This will save the spot for the machine when it is returned.

When storage space for equipment is limited, the librarian may wish to place equipment on permanent loan to individual departments. If the amount of use can be correctly anticipated, this will reduce clerical time required to move equipment in and out of the library.

DECISION SIX: Whether to place equipment in departments.

The following three factors should be considered:

- Security

Care must be taken to protect equipment from loss, theft, or vandalism. Supply companies have heavy tie-down straps that can lock equipment to furniture. Special covers can be locked over equipment to discourage removal of the cover and jamming of internal parts.

- Repairs

Ask users to report any malfunctions. Frequent review of the functioning of equipment is needed to anticipate repairs. Equipment placed on loan to departments should be returned to the library when it does not work and at least once a year for preventative maintenance.

- Uncertainty of use

Equipment not under your direct jurisdiction may be little used in one department though it would be heavily used in another. Also, one person in a department may monopolize equipment, keeping it from other users. Materials requiring equipment will be little used when it becomes difficult to get equipment. Whether in the library or elsewhere, equipment should be regularly monitored for use.

The purpose of this chapter has been to outline some general management tasks and to explain why libraries are so carefully organized. Chapter 4 discusses the circulation of materials and equipment.

GLOSSARY

Bibliographic database. A database containing records that describe or list the items owned by the library.

Card catalog. Drawers of 3-by-5-inch cards that index the holdings of a library.

Citation. A reference that identifies the source, such as a book or magazine article, from which a quote or idea is taken.

Classification. A code for arranging materials on library shelves by subject.

Online public access catalog (OPAC). A computerized index to a library, usable by patrons.

Preprocessed item. A book or audiovisual item that comes shelf ready from a dealer, i.e., with catalog cards, spine label, plastic jacket, and borrower's card.

Subject headings. Words used as filing terms in an index. For example, the word CATS may be selected as a subject heading rather than FELINES.

Weeding. Choosing items to delete from a library collection.

Chapter 2

USERS IN THE LIBRARY

This chapter focuses on patrons who actually come into your facility, rather than those who may request information through interlibrary loan or other out-of-library use. Users come when they

- know that they need information.
- know that information is available in your library.
- find a warm welcome when they enter.
- feel welcome while they are there.
- locate what they need easily.
- receive willing help from staff.
- are able to use what they find in a comfortable facility.
- are satisfied with what is available to help them.

The number of actual users is based on the number of potential users in any library area. Your clientele is defined by many parameters, including geographic area, political area, school district boundary, employment by a corporation, or membership in a congregation, among others.

IDENTIFYING THE COMMUNITY

The relationship of potential users to actual users depends on how well the facility meets the needs of the community. Potential patrons must know the content of the collection and which services are offered. Whether they find anything to help them depends on what you know or can learn about the community, so that you can plan programs, buy materials, and offer services that will be appealing. Your correct analysis of the community may determine whether a potential user becomes a satisfied client.

ACTION ONE: Analyze the community.

For corporate and school libraries, the "community" is closed. That is, the clientele is in-house, and the population of the community is relatively small. You need only learn the names of those who will need these services and meet with them to ask them what they expect from you.

In the school setting, you will determine the following:

- What the teachers teach
- At what grade levels they teach
- When each curriculum area is taught during the semester
- The number of students taught
- What texts, if any, are used

If you determine the level of parental interest in the school, you can predict the interest they may have in the education of their children. Is there an active parent organization? Do parents volunteer to work at the school? How large is an audience at a performance presented by students?

A public library serves a geographic, politically, or legally defined area. Anyone not living in the area may be refused service or asked to pay a fee to use the library. When this is true, confirmation of address through driver's license or other means may be required from prospective users.

Knowing the education level of the community is helpful in planning services. It has been shown that college graduates are more often library users. If the library is in a blue collar area, you may need to acquaint the community with the library or offer different services to encourage use of the collection. Determining the number of children in each area and the locations of day care centers or other programs and public and private schools will help you decide where to have story hours. Choices can include the library building itself or alternate locations such as day care centers or summer playground program facilities.

In the corporate library, you will find out who needs information, in what form, and for what purpose. You may not need to purchase any books or magazines. Rather, the total service may be provided from online databases. Although employees may be interested in a leisure reading collection, the first priority will be to support company research information needs, from airline routes to chemical formulas, addresses for suppliers to manufacturing statistics.

The small church library is often used only by minister(s) and its Sunday school teachers. If this is true, you will work closely with them to be sure you have the information needed to prepare sermons and lessons for classes. Other church libraries provide both religious and secular materials for adults and children.

This has been a very brief discussion of conducting a community analysis. Please review the suggested readings in the bibliography for more assistance.

NUMBER OF USERS

Library services and programs are designed for specific audiences. This section will help you count the users. There are three types: primary, secondary, and potential. Primary users are the regular, continuing audience for library services. Secondary audiences include those who have access to the library services and collection but are not a part of the immediate community. Potential users are part of the audience for library services but are in reality nonusers, using the library irregularly if at all. They could and should be regular users, and their lack of use becomes a focus of a nonuser study.

Primary audiences include children and teachers in a school, citizens of a community, employees of a corporation, or members of a congregation. Secondary users are parents of children in the school, citizens of other communities who pay a yearly borrower's fee, or persons who access any collection in-house but do not take materials away from the premises.

The number of potential users related to the number of actual users varies by type of library. In elementary schools, most potential users are actual users. School use, particularly at the elementary level, is often regularized by the school schedule, and all children visit weekly with their classes. Individual students and small groups come at other times, and use will show 100 percent of potential users visiting the library one or more times each week. In other elementary schools, schedules are flexible, with students coming on an as-needed basis.

Public libraries, open to all residents, are used regularly by a smaller percentage of potential patrons, as are libraries in churches and corporations. Public libraries usually require registration, with proof of local address, after which a borrower's card is issued. The number of registered borrowers is a second number to count. A third number includes the patrons who actually come to the library and check out materials. A fourth number of users are those who telephone with a reference question. Although they might not be residents of the community or registered borrowers, they are among the library users.

Potential patrons in a corporation are all those who work in the corporation. However, not all occupations within the corporation require research. Also, when collections in corporate libraries emphasize particular divisions of the company, use will be uneven. Use is also uneven when services offered by the corporation library must be charged back to the departments or sections.

As stated above, church libraries provide materials for a primary audience of the clergy and the teachers. Members of the congregation occasionally use the collection and its devotional materials, but they will be less likely to be considered primary users.

Primary and secondary audiences are easily identified and can be counted through their presence in libraries. Use can also be calculated by counting circulation of items and by reference questions answered. Users can be queried about their satisfaction with services and their wishes for additional materials or services.

Determining the numbers of nonusers and their reasons for not using the library requires much more effort on your part, and this topic will be discussed later in this section when we discuss public relations.

FEELING WELCOME

You represent the library to everyone you meet, both inside and outside the facility. Often the tasks to be accomplished on any given day may seem overwhelming, and it is difficult to greet users with a smile and ask, "What can I do for you?" Responding to user needs should take precedence over other tasks, such as materials to be shelved, answering correspondence, and orders to be sent. Patrons should be treated as if their request is the highest priority for the day. In fact, one can never be sure that any request is not going to result in a major breakthrough—whether it is from kindergartner or the CEO of the corporation. The best way to encourage use and retain users is to have a user-friendly library.

DECISION ONE: To insure a user-friendly library.

Enthusiasm is contagious. Greeting patrons with a smile, standing if one is sitting, and all other affirmative body language gestures indicate that the library is a welcome spot for all who enter. No facility, no matter how attractively arranged or decorated, can withstand the presence of perpetually unhappy, unfriendly, less welcoming staff members.

ACTION ONE: Model user-friendly behavior.

Your example of user-friendly behavior will serve as a constant reminder to other staff that the patron comes first. This attitude begins with your first day in the library and continues until a new librarian replaces you. If staff who are there when you arrive have a different perception of their priorities, it becomes your first order of business at the first staff meeting to explain the concept of friendly behavior.

ACTION TWO: Check staff serving patrons frequently.

It is your responsibility to confirm staff attitudes when they are serving patrons to see that their behavior conforms to library policy of friendly behavior.

ACTION THREE: Encourage stressed staff to take brief breaks.

When you or your staff feel an attack of unfriendly behavior coming on, it is time to take a break. Often, just knowing that such an opportunity is available will prevent regrettable behavior. At other times, it is imperative that you and your staff stop and take a moment to regroup.

Once you have made patrons feel that their library is a friendly place and they are welcome there, they can be made aware of the full range of services. Although you plan services to meet their needs, they must be acquainted with these services if they are to use them.

AWARENESS OF SERVICES OFFERED

This section covers public relations activities for present services and new services. Finally, suggestions are made for ways to find out why some potential patrons do not use the library.

Public Relations

Regular users come to libraries because they know about services provided for them and understand what is available to help them pursue their information needs. Nonusers also must be made aware of the library. In some cases, users are required to come to the library. For instance, students in elementary and secondary schools have teachers who bring them to the library for assigned class periods, but most other librarians must devise methods to entice users to their libraries. Potential patrons need compelling reasons to come if they are to become regular users. An aggressive public relations campaign may be needed to make potential users aware of services and benefits offered to them.

A variety of books is available to assist in planning public relations activities. They may begin with such simple activities as the following:

- Creating attractive bulletin boards and other displays
- Mailing newsletters
- Explaining new services
- Reacquainting clientele with underused services
- Providing lists of new materials
- Promoting contests
- Providing bookmarks
- Posting and mailing flyers

All of these encourage use. You can also distribute "current awareness" lists or brochures about items of interest in current magazines. Many ways exist to draw attention to the library. Simple actions are effective means to change potential users into users.

Sometimes, however, you may need more elaborate campaigns. For more detailed public relations suggestions, you can peruse works by public relations experts who discuss how to sell any number of products with expensive campaigns, including billboards and television advertising. Some of these can be found in the annotated bibliography. Glitzy promotions can make it difficult for even the most reluctant users to resist being drawn into your library.

Public relations activities can be used not only to make clientele aware of present services but also to promote new services.

New Services

New services are planned when you are aware of patron needs, when new items or technologies become available, and when new resources are added to collections. As you learn the needs of users, you can begin to plan services to meet their needs. Services will be discussed in chapter 6. They are mentioned here in relation to users, because new services might be needed to fulfill the various requirements of your clientele, as well as to attract nonusers to the library.

Reaching the Nonuser

As stated above, much can be done to increase public awareness of your library. You will need to decide how much success is practical. A single person running a library with no help may find that use is heavy, and additional users would be the straw that breaks the camel's back. However, when the library seems to be missing a segment of clients who should be using the library, an awareness campaign is in order.

Nonuse of any library is based on a wide variety of factors, including the following:

- Perceptions of potential patrons

Patrons bring their views of all libraries with them when they come into yours. Because you probably do not have their library experience history, you must learn those perceptions. In fact, they may have no perceptions at all. When a child is not taken to the public library for story hour, or when the school had no library, the adult may not understand that visiting an information center can be a rewarding experience.

- Negative feelings generated when patrons found too many restrictions on library use

You should also be aware that when children are prohibited from taking materials because of their age or when their parents are concerned about possible fines for overdue items, negative feelings begin at an early age. When children are banned from the adult collection, it may cause them to feel resentful that parts of all libraries are restricted to them. Further, patrons who have gone into libraries where staff treat their requests as interruptions or do not even look up from the desk will not readily seek out your library.

- Lack of knowledge about what the library has to offer

One indication that persons are literate is that they know they need information. Nonusers who have little experience with library use may not know that they need information, and if they do, they may not recognize the potential assistance they can get from the library.

- Finding poor resources or none at all in the library

Patrons who seldom find what they need or who find the materials are too simple, too hard, out-of-date, or irrelevant will not be interested in returning to a library.

- Little help from librarians when they do visit

Persons who visit unfamiliar places need to be made comfortable. They need to feel that they belong there, that they know what to do while they are there, and that they have a reason for being there. Librarians who are helpful will make patrons welcome, help them find items, and make their visit successful and useful.

An even darker picture is drawn when a potential user has had no library service at all. Some persons grow up in rural areas where no public library exists and the school library, if one exists, is in the high school and managed only part-time by the English teacher. Little attention was paid to the collection or its use. If these persons went to college, they were unlikely to use the academic library unless they were taken there and given an assignment to be completed while they were there.

All of the above are hypothetical situations that may fit some of your patrons, but probably not all. You should find out exactly who your nonusers are and why they are not using your library.

DECISION TWO: To conduct a nonuser survey.

You can ask those persons who should be using your library why they do not do so. If you know why they are not patrons, then you can better decide how to reach them with services.

ACTION ONE: Decide how and where you will collect information.

A survey form used in a previous study (see appendix A) can be a starting point to help you develop questions. Interviewing possible clients is another way to discover their previous library use patterns and their interests.

Survey forms are designed to reach the appropriate audience, and where that audience is located varies. Where they are determines how to reach them. For example:

School: Place survey forms in teachers' mail boxes.

Public Library: Stand with clipboard and survey form at a busy intersection and ask passersby to respond to questions.

Corporation: Insert survey forms in paycheck envelopes.

Church: Publish survey in church newsletter.

ACTION TWO: Determine what you will collect.

Explain the purpose of the survey at the top of the form or at the beginning of the survey interview. First, ask yourself what you really need to know. This often varies from what you might like to know. If you ask for unnecessary information, you will lose time in tabulating the responses. If you want better answers, questions should be worded with great care, so that they are correctly interpreted and understood by the responder. Answers must be understood by the questioner, or the information gathered will be incorrectly interpreted. Check the sample survey form in appendix A.

ACTION THREE: Determine what you will do with the answers.

Once you have the answers, determine if expressed needs can be fulfilled by making users aware of services and information already available in your collection. When you can satisfy user needs by securing information from outside locations, advertise this service. When new materials are needed, order them and advertise their arrival in the library. In the latter case, a selection decision is made, as discussed in chapter 7.

Often patrons' needs require a new service. When a new service is implemented, priority ranking is given to present services, and decisions are made about reallocating duties of staff. Services to be offered are sometimes limited by the skills and expertise of the staff. As new services are created and staff are trained to provide these services, patrons must be reminded of their existence, just as they are introduced to current but little used services.

STAFF ASSIGNMENTS RELATED TO USERS

In most small libraries, you are the only person on the staff. When materials in your library are heavily used, basic services such as the following take most of your time:

- Helping patrons locate materials

- Answering questions from the reference collection

- Keeping a record of materials being circulated

- Re-shelving materials as they are returned

When this is true, you have only your own personal attitude of helpfulness to maintain. When additional paid staff are available, they are trained to reflect a service concept and a pleasure at serving patrons. As discussed above, staff must maintain an attitude of willingness to assist all patrons all of the time. You and your staff members can help each other, so that slippage in the positive approach to patrons is minimized.

Volunteers are sometimes available to supplement paid staff. Usually, they do so because they are somehow related to the users. That is, their children attend the school, they are members of a service organization dedicated to supporting this community project, or they are members of the congregation. When volunteers work in an area with patrons, they are given careful instructions so that they understand not only the tasks they are assigned, but also their attitudes toward users. A manual explaining their tasks should also explain the need for confidentiality in their work in the library and their experiences with patron use of materials. More information on the management of staff and volunteers is given in chapter 3.

SCHEDULING HOURS OF THE LIBRARY

You may have little choice concerning when your library is open. However, when you do have options, you may wish to weigh the following considerations.

DECISION THREE: *When should your library be open?*

Your library should be open at times convenient to users. Obviously school libraries are most often open during the school day. Visits to the school library may be a means to provide preparation time for the teacher. Library visits will be planned around other activities such as art, music, and physical education classes. School bus arrivals and departures may hinder use of the library by students before and after school, just as the hours teachers are in the building will dictate when the librarian can open and close the library.

If an open or flexible schedule is available for the school library, a weekly sign-up sheet may be posted to allow teachers to choose a specific time to come to the library. When visits are not mandated by release time, the librarian may need to help teachers remember to bring their students, so that all children have regular access to the library. When scheduling is open, teachers are more often expected to remain with their classes in the library. Teachers must understand the importance of library visits, and they must be involved in planning for visits so that the time is considered valuable rather than filler or waste.

Patrons visit public libraries that are conveniently located and open at times when users are free to go to the library. This means your library is open when the major part of the user population, if not the entire community, is available to visit. Scheduling can limit access to those who should be encouraged to come. If most of the people in the community work or are in school, the library should be open in the evening; by contrast, a community of mostly retired persons will require more daytime hours. The survey form requesting information about why nonusers do not come to the library could include questions about preferred times to use the library.

Visits to church libraries coincide with other activities of a congregation. Having the library open only during rather than before and after Sunday morning church services would seriously limit use. Certainly few churches can have libraries open long hours, but hours can be scheduled so that the library is available to the maximum number of users at times convenient for them. The minister and the church secretary can help set hours until the preferences of others in the congregation have been determined.

Corporation libraries are open during the working day. Use will be made when the need for information arises, and this should most often be when employees are in offices and on the job. Electronic mail queries can be left overnight, in a sense making the service 24 hours a day.

DECISION FOUR: What happens when you are not there?

One consideration for expanding the hours of any library is granting access at times when the library is locked to most users. In situations where you are available only part-time, other access is required if materials are to be available when needed. In the case of the school library, you are given few options for locking or unlocking the library. Teachers and students are allowed full access by the principal, even if you would prefer it to be left closed when you are away. Or, the principal may limit access to the library though you would prefer that it be left open.

When the school library is open at all times, you might choose students to assume the role of acting librarian. Teach them to see that materials are checked out correctly and items returned are checked in before being renewed or checked to another student. Although training helpers will not insure total accuracy of your system, it will greatly alleviate errors and help you to keep materials circulating.

Public libraries must have supervision whenever the doors are unlocked. Any replacements or substitutes for permanent staff need a well-designed manual to answer their questions and to address unusual situations. A directory of safety officials such as police, fire department, and hospitals must be readily accessible.

Corporation and church libraries need well-organized circulation systems that work when the room is left open without supervision. Each situation will be handled differently, but the goal is to maintain access while balancing security needs.

In any situation, you may be expected to keep the facility locked and only opened by users who have your permission to gain access. You will then decide to whom you will provide keys or grant permission to open the door.

ACTION ONE: Determine who needs access.

When you are responsible for the maintenance of the library facility, it is difficult to choose just who should have access when you are not there. If users do not abide by some system of check out and return, it will not take long for you to have a very small collection in the library and a much larger collection "lost" in classrooms, offices, and homes. Users with access to the library at times when it is not open for supervised service must be convinced that they have a responsibility to help you maintain the records of items borrowed from the collection.

SIZE AND MAINTENANCE OF THE FACILITY

It is most likely that you will inherit your facilities, rather than be asked to plan new facilities, make major changes, or secure larger spaces. What you can do is view the facility as a user would see it and determine what changes are needed to make it more appealing and easier to use. Facilities should truly welcome the user.

The most visible area of any library is the main room, usually called the reading room. Pictures, posters, plants, displays, and other means are used to sell the library to the patron upon entering. Materials should be displayed so they can be easily seen by browsers. The furniture should be attractive, with fabrics and color whenever practical. The furniture can also invite the patron by being comfortably arranged.

Consideration should be given to division of quiet and less quiet areas. Two areas that are often noisier are the circulation and reference desks. Patrons coming to use materials placed on reserve, find materials, return materials, and check out materials, are seldom silent, nor do you want them to be. That is an excellent time to discuss how well the material meets needs, to find out additional needs of the patron, and to build good public relations. This area should be near the entrance, so that patrons with shorter errands can conduct their business and leave without disturbing users who are quietly working on projects or reading.

By its nature, a reference area is for asking and answering questions. Patrons need as much opportunity as possible to decide their search needs if you are going to help them, and the ensuing conversations must be above a whisper to be understood.

Placement of tables, chairs, and shelving can decrease noise by separating readers and researchers from browsers and others just looking for recreational materials. Placement of shelves can also help you monitor use of the library. You should consider the following:

- Tall shelving placed where it will not obstruct a supervising eye

It is more likely that unexpected events can occur when patrons can hide in any area of the library, obstructed from view by tall shelves.

- Low shelves to divide areas of the library for different uses, e.g., quiet, noisy, reference, word processing
- Tables and chairs separated by low shelving to minimize conversations in areas that should be quiet

You also must provide visual directions to various areas of the library to improve access to information. Users need the following:

- Records of what the library owns: the card catalog, or the online public access catalog

- Signage to help them find materials

- Open shelves and easily accessible filing cabinets

- Comfortable and well-lighted seating at desks, tables, leisure areas

Seating should be comfortable so that researchers can spread out their work. The time has come to make provisions for users with laptop computers. Other patrons will expect the library to provide word-processing, online searching, desktop publishing, and photocopying capabilities, among others.

But what do your users actually need? Matching activities of users to the facility may require a planned review of the facility.

DECISION FIVE: To review the library facility.

Rearranging a library facility improves access and can often solve discipline or noise problems or traffic congestion. If a problem has not been addressed, reviewing the facility helps you focus on a solution. Even when major problems have not surfaced, changing locations for items will bring them to the attention of potential users. Reviewing the arrangement of the library helps you analyze traffic flow and other housing functions.

ACTION ONE: Sketch the arrangement of the library.

- Are noisy areas as separate from quiet areas as possible?

- Are tables and chairs at a convenient height for most patrons?

- Is it possible to see patrons when they are at tables?

- Are shelves at a convenient height for most patrons?

- Is it possible to see patrons when they are at the shelves?

ACTION TWO: Check the traffic pattern.

- Can patrons move in and out of the library easily?

- Can patrons move through the library with ease?

ACTION THREE: Check the ambiance.

- Is the library appealing?

- Is signage adequate?

TECHNOLOGY IN THE FACILITY

Information is found in books and magazines as well as the more traditional nonprint media—films, videos, filmstrips, recordings, and microforms. But technologies are constantly expanding. The day is past when the library could function with a single communication line into the facility. Many patrons have modems in their offices and at home. Through electronic mail, fax, online databases, and bibliographic utilities, information can flow easily in and out of your library. These complement the telephone used for voice conversations.

DECISION SIX: What technologies are needed?

Analyze where you find most of the basic information your users request. Is it a print format? Microfiche and CD-ROM? Audiovisual? Online? Interlibrary loan?

When you are unfamiliar with what information is available in what formats using which technologies, a professional librarian can help you understand the latest formats used to provide information. They are aware of technologies that can be used easily by patrons themselves and which you or your staff will need to be responsible for searching. It is time to ▥**Ask a Librarian**.

ACTION ONE: What technologies are for direct use by patrons?

Consider placing technologies where users have easy access if they are expected to manipulate the technology. As card catalogs become computer stations and CD-ROM terminals become commonplace, facilities must change to accommodate these technologies. Users will bring their own laptop computers to use in the library, or they may anticipate word-processing and desktop publishing capabilities with in-house PCs.

ACTION TWO: Where do you place technologies not available for open access?

Equipment with long-distance devices, such as modems and fax machines, permits access to communication links that are directly billed to the library. In order to budget for such use, searches are limited to the staff rather than open to patrons. When this happens, the technology needs to be placed in a less accessible location, or a password system established before a charge can be incurred.

In conclusion, users have been identified, nonusers have been queried, and the facility reviewed for ambiance, signage, and ease of access. Full access to all information held in the library has been promoted. The next chapter covers the management, roles, and responsibilities of all persons working in libraries and information centers, whether paid or volunteer.

Chapter 3

STAFFING THE LIBRARY

This chapter will present the role of a single person staffing the library either part-time or full-time. How to manage paid staff and volunteers is discussed, and suggestions are included for working with management.

WORKING ALONE

For the librarian working solo, discussion of managing personnel may seem unnecessary. When a single person has full responsibility for the operation of a library, the job description is a single word: Everything.

When this is true, you analyze your job description and assign a percentage of time to be spent on each task. In this way, you can assign priorities for activities in the library. An example of basic tasks matched to percentage of time to be allocated is shown in figure 3.1, on page 28.

Translated into a daily schedule, a day that begins at 9:00 A.M. and ends at 5:00 P.M., with a 30-minute lunch and two 15-minute breaks, would find you spending roughly 4 hours on reference, 40 minutes on management, 40 minutes on circulation and re-shelving, and 21 minutes each on processing, selecting, correspondence, and public relations.

It is unlikely that any work day would fit neatly into such arbitrary time slots. Nonetheless, consideration of the amount of time that could or should be allocated to tasks helps put expenditures of time into a perspective. When helping patrons has the highest priority (and it should); the reality of spending two hours on circulating and re-shelving materials rather than the 40 minutes allocated indicates a need for additional help. When processing materials takes an hour each day, clerical help, preprocessed materials, and a more automated system to record additions are needed.

To reemphasize, you would be unlikely to establish a schedule that said every day, from 9:00 A.M. to 9:41 A.M., I will plan; from 9:41 A.M. to 2:41 P.M., I will do reference; from 2:41 P.M. to 3:01 P.M., I will select; and from 3:01 P.M. to 3:22 P.M., I will process. Yet, if your entire day is spent circulating and re-shelving materials, adjustments are needed. Further suggestions for evaluating use of time will be discussed in chapter 8.

Sample Tasks and Time Allocations
One-Person Library

Percent (%)	Task
60	Reference, including
	assisting patrons
	photocopying materials
	requests for information from other libraries
	database searching
5	Processing materials
5	Selecting new materials
10	Circulating materials and re-shelving returned materials
5	Correspondence (including orders for new materials)
10	Management, including
	planning meetings with administrators
	training volunteers
5	Public relations
————	outreach
100	in-house (bulletin boards, display cases)
	newsletters, new acquisitions lists

Fig. 3.1. Sample tasks and time allocations in a one-person library.

WHEN YOU WORK ONLY PART-TIME

Although full-time management of a library is difficult to undertake with little training, being limited to part-time responsibilities is even more troublesome. If your only part-time role is as library manager, you may find yourself working more and more hours within the "part-time" job description and salary scale. If you adhere rigidly to your part-time hours, less time is available to discover mistakes, learn from mistakes, make adjustments, and test whether a new method is more or less successful. You will have little opportunity to plan your schedule because you will be busy trying to manage the library and meet the needs of any other part-time assignments you may have.

When your management is part-time and you have no other responsibilities, you schedule the library hours to match user needs within the number of hours you are expected to work. When your assignment is part-time library and part-time elsewhere, even out of the building, your library hours are secondary to other tasks deemed more important by you or your administrators.

Different management roles are needed with regard to libraries that are left open and libraries that are closed. If you are the only person working in the library, what happens when you are not there? A library left open without supervision may suffer loss of materials and equipment, the contents left in disarray, and misuse of materials and equipment.

If the library is in a church, possible users may not be as numerous as in other types of libraries. By contrast, the public library cannot be left unattended for even the shortest period of time. In school or special libraries, most persons intend to be honest, but it is much faster to leave the library without checking out materials than to go through the process required to do so, even running a light pen across the bar code. Most persons have every intention of returning what they have borrowed, but it is easy to forget that one has an item, much less remember to return it. With no record of the checkout, it is difficult for the librarian to trace the borrower.

Equipment may be an even more costly loss, and the loss may be to persons not connected with the agency. While equipment can be stolen from buildings when they are locked for the night, leaving a room unattended may increase daylight forays into the equipment collection.

Because most users have little idea of the actual arrangement in libraries, they maybe unable to replace correctly materials they have borrowed. They may place returned materials on shelves or in file cabinets without giving credit to the returnee. If many items are used, the part-time librarian may be overwhelmed with the numbers to be checked in and returned to the shelves before they can be checked out again.

When no one is available to oversee use, materials and equipment are likely to be misused. Items may be destroyed if something goes wrong with the equipment and there is no one there to correct the problem.

When the library is locked while you are away, you must be concerned with what patrons may need and cannot get. In schools, special libraries, and churches, you may need to move some materials to classrooms or office areas while you are not there.

Part-time management makes it essential to plan your time while you are in the library. Keeping a schedule in priority order of what needs to be done and where you are on the way to completion of each activity will save time in trying to decide each day where to begin, or, even more frustrating, where you left off in the sequence of steps.

A novice beginning a part-time assignment should undertake one or two services rather than try to offer the full range. Doing one or two things well will be more rewarding than not being able to accomplish many. If you are in this position, it would be well to ▢**Ask a Librarian** for help at the beginning.

PAID STAFF

If another person is available to assist in the library, you check both your job description and that of your assistant or assistants. All aspects of the operation must be included, and care should be taken to see that professional tasks are assigned to you and clerical tasks to the assistant or assistants. When job descriptions exist, these are checked to see that all tasks necessary for the smooth operation of library services are included.

When no job descriptions exist, these should be developed with the duties needed to insure that daily library functions are covered between the librarian and staff. You will assign to clerical personnel the tasks such as re-shelving materials, circulation of items, ordering and processing new materials, correspondence, and bookkeeping, among others. An example of basic tasks matched to percentage of time to be allocated is shown in figure 3.2 on page 30.

**Sample Tasks and Time Allocations
Two-Person Library**

Percent	Staff	Task
20	M	Reference, including
10	M	assisting patrons
10	C	photocopying materials
10	C	requests for information from other libraries
30	M	database searching
10	C	Processing materials
15	M	Selecting new materials
5	M	Circulating materials
40	C	Circulating materials and re-shelving returned materials
30	C	Correspondence, including orders for new materials
10	M	Management, including
		planning meetings with administrators
		training volunteers
10	M	Public relations
		outreach
		in-house (bulletin boards, display cases
		newsletters, acquisitions lists

Total 200%

M = manager   C = clerk

Fig. 3.2. Sample tasks and time allocations in a two-person library.

One telling argument for the addition of clerical staff is the relationship of clerical duties and salary compared to your responsibility for those tasks and the other duties that will not be accomplished because some clerical duties must be completed if the library collection is to remain at the disposal of users. Clerical staff should not be expected to carry out duties requiring the expertise the apprentice librarian acquires, and managers should not regularly complete clerical tasks. In some situations, this may be mandated.

When staffing school library media centers, care should be taken to follow state laws concerning who is responsible for students coming to the library. State regulations often require a certified teacher-librarian be with students at all times. Library media staff who are not certified should not be assigned responsibility for children when no certified person is with them.

It is hoped that you will have paid staff, because using volunteers is not a permanent substitute. When paid staff are part of the library, you may have responsibility for selecting staff unless your agency has a personnel office in charge of new hires. When you become responsible for hiring and dismissal of staff, you become a personnel manager.

Hiring

Rules for hiring may be related to a union contract or hiring policy for your agency. When steps to employment are carefully defined but are not solely the responsibility of a personnel office, you must put this information in your procedures manual, with copies of application forms and indications of personnel information to be requested. This will help you follow the necessary hiring process. When no formal process exists, you should establish a mechanism and record the steps to follow in your procedures manual.

DECISION ONE: To hire additional staff members or replace staff members who have left.

The following steps are taken: communicate with potential applicants, meet applicants, and choose a new employee from a list of applicants.

You will need to place an advertisement in the newspaper or a notice on a personnel department bulletin board, or make an announcement to a church congregation.

ACTION ONE: Place an ad.

The advertisement briefly describes the competencies expected from any applicant. Most potential applicants will be interested in tasks, educational requirements, specific skills needed, and salary. Sample ads are shown below:

Ad 1—Library Assistant

Assistant will check materials in and out using automated circulation control system; interface with serials control system; process orders for new materials and equipment; enter data for online catalog; fill interlibrary loan requests; and other duties such as filing, shelving, inventory. Minimum of two years of college. Salary: $00,000-00,000 with excellent benefits. Send resume to:

Ad 2—Administrative Assistant

Seeking a highly motivated person with proven administrative skills to work in information agency. Applicants should have 1-3 years administration and experience with PCs (word processing, spreadsheet, E-mail preferred). Applicants should have strong organizational skills, good interpersonal communication skills, must be able to work on several tasks simultaneously with minimal supervision, and must be prepared to meet the public. Apply to:

Ad 3—Clerical

Religious organization seeks general clerical help. Position is full-time, starting at $0.00 per hr. Duties to include typing, filing, some answering phones. Apply to:

Ad 4—Educational Aide

Position open for candidates who enjoy working with children. Some typing (PC word processing preferred) and must be willing to learn new technology. Send resume to:
  J. Johnson, Title
  Name of Library
  Street Address
  City, State, ZIP

Although ads are short, you must know exactly what skills and behavior you expect, so that respondents can be given accurate responses to their inquiries about the position. Anyone who will work in an information environment must like working with others on both short- and long-term projects. They must have pleasant personalities and established interpersonal skills. When technology is available or inevitable, they must be skilled in use of a variety of technologies, so that you are not required to see that they overcome any resistance they might have to using any piece of equipment. If a major responsibility is to handle vendors and problems with orders, you will confirm their experience working with suppliers.

If you prefer to train someone with little experience, confirming their service concept may be all that is required. However, if expertise is essential, you must make sure you have decided exactly what that expertise is, so that your review of credentials and your questions in the interview process correctly elicit this information.

ACTION TWO: Applicants complete the application form.

As stated above, an agency may have a prescribed application form. If no application exists, the ones offered in appendix B may be used as a beginning point to provide basic data. Your specific needs may be added.

ACTION THREE: Review application forms.

References are called for those persons who meet the requirements for the position. You should not make the mistake of accepting only the contents of a reference letter. Telephone calls must be made to those persons named as references. The litigious fears of most persons today are such that it is unlikely that referees will write any negative comments; however, most persons are willing to discuss deficiencies or possible problems verbally. Applicants who receive a favorable review from their referees are then asked to come for an interview.

ACTION FOUR: Interview applicants.

In some situations, you may be expected to establish a limited list of interview questions to ask each applicant. This is often true of government positions. In others, the interviewer asks a series of extemporaneous questions in order to determine the best fit between applicant and job description. Questions may include the following:

- What about the ad interested you?
- What did you like best about any of your previous jobs?
- What do you like best about your current job?
- What don't you like about your current job?
- Why do you think you want to work here?

Be sure to allow applicants time to ask you questions about their expectations. An applicant whose only inquiries concern vacation time and sick leave policy may be more interested in time off the job than time on the job.

Once you have completed the interview process, you will weigh the qualifications of each applicant against the job description. Next you will want to determine how each particular applicant would fit into the workplace from the standpoint of the work and from the standpoint of the interpersonal relationships there. From these considerations, you choose an employee.

ACTION FIVE: Introduce employee to library. New employees must be oriented to the library.

- Review the job description to confirm that assigned tasks are understood in their general context.
- Discuss items in the procedures manual, emphasizing tasks that are the responsibility of the new hire.
- Explain sick leave and vacation policies if these are not outlined elsewhere.
- Present general and specific expectations of as many aspects of job performance as are practical in the available time.
- Review policies and procedures with the new employee daily, or after the person has been on the job no more than two weeks. Take time to answer any follow-up questions.
- Plan tasks for the new person to do immediately.

As procedures are followed, information that was not presented or understood in the initial orientation can be explained. It is unlikely that you will be able to anticipate all possible misunderstandings on the part of the new hire or that your new worker will be able to grasp all situations the first day on the job.

The manager, especially in a small operation, must be prepared to respond to questions and to explain fully, so that all employees understand their rights and your expectations of their performance.

You obviously present your agency in the best possible light. Applicants who wish to become employed will also be exhibiting the most positive view of their candidacy. Responses to oral questions must be carefully weighed against items reported on the application form. In cases of unanswered questions, former employers may also be queried about the job performance of any potential employee.

When You and Your Staff Do Not Get Along

The employment process is difficult. Applicants who appear to be a perfect match may not fit into the routines and interpersonal relations of your library. What seems to be an ideal match for the applicant could also fail to meet that person's expectations, and the employee quits. If not, the situation usually becomes troublesome, because you must then encourage the employee to change positions or you may be required to initiate dismissal procedures. In either case, when an employee leaves the position, you must face training the new hire. Dismissal procedures are discussed further in "Evaluating Staff Performance" on pages 35-36.

Inheriting

A staff member who is in place when you arrive should know a great deal about the functioning of your library. When this person is in a clerical position and has been working in the library for some time with no supervision, the assistant may feel more qualified to conduct the business of the library than someone just coming on board. You may be overseeing someone who has applied for the position that you have received. In all cases, good interpersonal relations are needed to turn these colleagues into friends and co-workers.

The following four steps can help ease this process:

- Learn as much as you can by asking both how and why the library functions the way it does.

You should learn the present processes and analyze the degree of success or failure before advocating change.

- Discuss problems in the functioning of activities.

This allows the inherited employee to suggest ways to improve any process and to learn your ideas for improvements. Change is much easier if everyone has had a say in the planning, understands why, and buys into both the need for a new procedure and the probable outcome of the procedure being proposed.

- Compliment employees when suggestions are accepted.

It is especially gratifying for staff to be included in the applause when improvements are successful.

- Listen carefully to explanations.

Veteran employees may exhibit attitudes that tell you when resistance to change is just resistance to change or if the new method might not work in the present situation or at this particular time. Existing equipment, staff, or facility arrangement may pose problems that are not immediately obvious, and veteran staff members may be able to point out both problems and solutions to your anticipated changes. Changes often have unintended effects; when you move the microfiche reader, the cabinet holding fiche may hold other items that have now been removed from proximity to their indexes.

It is most likely that you will function in a small library with little staff. The working relationships will be close for many reasons; however, a primary case is that the actual facility is small. When there are few staff members, communication and interaction are frequent. If the relationships are adversarial, it will be apparent to your clientele and your administration. Cooperative relationships will be equally noted by library users.

Training

Staff newly hired may have the same preconceived notions of libraries as the population at large. They may think the position is one of circulation and be surprised at the amount of technology with which they must work. Those who need additional skills can learn these elsewhere if funds are allocated for workshops and release or compensatory time is granted.

One excellent training device is sending staff to visit similar libraries to see how they function. An employee who has begun to grasp the functions can visit a counterpart in another location to ask questions, see the operation, and learn better and more efficient ways to accomplish tasks.

EVALUATING STAFF PERFORMANCE

A performance appraisal of employees evaluates their job-related performance over a specified period of time. These evaluations must be as objective as possible. Data are collected concerning performance so that you can write an evaluation, assign a rating, discuss your analysis with the employee, and plan follow-up procedures to be conducted before the next formal evaluation.

During the interview at the time of hiring, performance expectations were outlined. At this initial evaluation, you and your employee continue to clarify assignments and job performance. Uncertainty concerning expectations can increase anxiety and decrease efficiency.

When employees are not completing job assignments in a timely fashion, they must be made aware of the problems and be given a chance to improve. Additional time is spent helping them understand expectations, so that an unfavorable review will not be a total surprise.

When an employee is meeting and exceeding expectations, this can happily be reported. You can further use this opportunity to build self-esteem, applaud good performance, and express gratitude for loyalty and good service.

Throughout the time between evaluations, data are collected and notes written. Examples of effective performance and areas for improvement are recorded. When an employee's performance is not at a high enough standard for retention, data collected must be specific and events confirmed by day and time. Whenever possible, performance should be observed by others whose names are also recorded in case you need to be substantiated.

Evaluation of staff is never comfortable for anyone, even good staff being reviewed by someone they respect and trust. That is why it is important that suggestions for improving performance and comments concerning improved performance be made throughout the time, so that staff know what is expected and understand why they are and are not meeting your expectations.

OTHER STAFF MEMBERS

Staff members who maintain the facility are called by several titles, including custodian, building engineer, and janitor. The person who maintains a facility has a great deal of effect on the operation. When pride is taken in this job, the cleanliness and orderliness of your library will be apparent to all who enter. These persons make the building shine, and the luster adds to an aura of efficiency (as well as to the ambiance). Constant appreciation of the high quality of performance given by custodians is essential.

Custodians can never be taken for granted. You must also take care to ask them to do only what is in the job description, particularly if union contracts dictate appropriate tasks and expected performance standards. When personnel believe they should be assigned only specified tasks, additional, unspecified activities such as making coffee in the morning may be "outside their job descriptions." However, they may be willing to perform such tasks if they are shared among yourself and other staff. Negative attitudes will result in a much less pleasant environment for all, while building positive attitudes among custodial staff increases the quality of your surroundings.

Technical staff may also be considered as other staff. They are crucial when information for patrons is available in communication resources requiring a wide variety of technologies. Technicians often receive higher salaries than other staff members because they command high salaries in the job market. Technicians may help train users for automation, or they may only be responsible for maintaining equipment in the center. Certainly, unless you want to learn how to repair equipment, you will value the services of your technical staff.

It is unlikely that you will be placed in complete charge of an entire building. More often, your library will be part of a larger system, whether in a school building, public library branch, church, or special library. For this reason, discussion of custodial staffing is covered, but maintenance and upkeep of a building are omitted here. When responsibility for a separate building is assigned to you, and you are responsible for maintenance of that building, **Ask a Librarian**.

A colleague can offer suggestions for electricians, plumbers, roofers, heating equipment, painters, and others to perform tasks beyond what is expected of the building maintenance staff.

VOLUNTEERS IN THE LIBRARY

As has been pointed out, you may be the only person to work in your library. When this is true, it is probable that you will become overwhelmed with tasks that you must repeat daily. You may believe you can serve more patrons if some of these tasks could be carried out by others, and you have a pool of ready and willing helpers. Even in situations where clerical staff are available, services can be expanded through the use of volunteers. You may decide to invite your willing helpers to assist in the library.

DECISION TWO: To use volunteers.

Volunteers can be helpful to any library program. Although they do not replace a paid employee with regular hours and designated assignments, volunteers can release you from some tasks.

ACTION ONE: Find out if volunteers are legal.

Some union members feel that free help delays an administrative decision to budget for a paid position. When this is the case, it may be illegal to accept the services of volunteers.

ACTION TWO: Decide which volunteers are most dependable.

Volunteers consider their first responsibility to be their primary role, such as care of their children. When this interferes with their volunteer service, you may be left without anticipated help.

Scheduling volunteers can be time-consuming. In schools and public libraries, a committee can be formed, and the committee chair becomes responsible for calling substitutes when a volunteer is unable to come at the assigned time.

ACTION THREE: Decide which tasks to assign.

Assignment of volunteers requires analyzing the tasks you wish to have them perform. These are matched to the ability of the volunteers. You can ask volunteers what they might like to do and discover an accomplished bulletin board artist, a desktop publishing expert, or a veteran storyteller.

ACTION FOUR: Train the volunteers.

- Analyze the level of knowledge of volunteers for a task.
- Demonstrate what should be done.
- Ask if they have any questions.
- Ask them to do the task one time and observe them.
- Ask if they have any questions.
- Review after a time to monitor their progress.
- Ask if they have any questions.
- Review their accomplishments at the end of the work period.

As an example, filing requires teaching filing rules and careful review of filing accomplished to confirm that the volunteer understood the rules and was able to follow them. Ideally, a single training session would prepare all volunteers to do these tasks. An alternative is to develop a guide for volunteers that explains tasks fully.

Volunteers usually work irregularly, and they will need frequent referral to your manual or a monthly reintroduction.

ACTION FIVE. *Assign appropriate tasks.*

Volunteers should be given tasks that deal only with general information. Only regular staff should have access to closed records such as confidential records of borrowers. Remind volunteers that they should not gossip about the activities of library patrons. Telling the neighborhood how many overdue books are in the hands of one patron is harmful.

ACTION SIX: *Monitor performance.*

Volunteers are helpful when they perform assigned tasks with accuracy. Their work should be checked to confirm that they have been able to complete the task assigned correctly.

ACTION SEVEN: *Applaud assistance.*

Volunteers are rewarded for their service. You express your thanks as they arrive and depart. In addition, a luncheon or tea may be planned to honor their service one or more times each year. If publicity can be placed in the local media, volunteers will be pleased to have the community recognition.

YOUNGER VOLUNTEERS IN THE LIBRARY

Young people may volunteer to work in your library. Student volunteers are often found in school libraries. In some schools, students are asked to do community service, and the school or public library may be a logical location for their service contribution. In other schools, actual credit may be given for student assistance in the library.

Boy Scouts and Girl Scouts may earn badges by working in a library. Their handbooks describe the duties they must accomplish, so you need to become familiar with these if you are in a school or public library.

The same need for confidentiality is apparent with young people who volunteer in libraries. Student workers should not be made aware of embarrassing situations that can be reported to other students.

Many librarians have been heard applauding the contributions made by their helpers. Volunteers can make extraordinary contributions to your program.

DIVISION OF TASKS IN THE LIBRARY

The author's father gave one piece of advice that managers should remember: "Never ask anyone to do anything you would not do yourself." Tasks that are boring for you may be equally or even more boring to your regular or volunteer staff. Think carefully about assignments, how long they will take, and how interesting they will be to the volunteer. For instance, it is not fun to file cards all day, or to do nothing but re-shelve materials. Divide the tasks based on what needs to be done and the ability of the volunteer to fit into the activities of the library while considering ways to make these tasks as attractive as possible. Allow the volunteer to work at a "fun" task after extended time at a less enjoyable assignment. Dividing tedious tasks into shorter periods of time with more exciting activities in between can help.

A second suggestion is to never ask others to do something they are not able to do. When the task is too difficult, the worker will be less than successful in the attempt, and no one will be pleased. It is a sure way to lose a volunteer or demoralize the staff. Expecting someone who is not artistic to change bulletin boards frequently will be frustrating for that person, and the effort could take more time and be less successful than a different task. Someone who knows nothing about writing or word processing will not want to help publish the newsletter.

WORKING WITH MANAGEMENT

Working with management is essential for the health of the library. If management is ignored, it is likely that the library will not be a high priority when budgets are developed. "Management" here is divided into "those who hired you" and "new kids on the block."

With Those Who Hired You

Although you tried to determine the agenda of management when you decided to accept the position, early on you need to confirm the accuracy of your perceptions. As you continue in your position, it is important to keep communication lines open to detect any changes in the following areas: philosophy, needs, perceptions, and, finally, budgeting practices.

- Philosophies may change.

Public controversy generated over intellectual freedom issues may weaken management's stance on a topic. It may be difficult to support you when members of your community question certain materials in the library. Board members may give in to strong political pressures.

- Needs may change.

You may have been hired to manage a book collection and find that you are now being asked to install automation systems to access wider information sources.

- Perceptions may change.

The image of the library can be enhanced by adding services, and this will encourage you to do so, although those services were not what you were hired to do. Through expanded services and excellent public relations, you can help improve any negative or erroneous perceptions of your governing board or administrators. They may have hired you to manage a book collection only to discover you have provided access to much wider information resources.

- Budgetary priorities may change.

Knowing as much as possible about everyone who has direct and indirect control over the budget will help you prepare to make the case for additional funding, new funding, or participating in projects with other departments, schools, or agencies. This will increase support for the library. Sharing in project proposals for additional funding, joint funding, and outside funding shows an interest in other departmental activities and helps you become acquainted with their interests, thereby making library services more supportive of their needs.

DECISION THREE: To maintain communication with administration.

As has been discussed, managing a library with a small staff means that you will do much of the work. However, day-by-day requests from patrons cannot distract you from the need to maintain communication with those who have responsibility over the library.

ACTION ONE: Meet as regularly as possible with administrators.

- Schedule appointments when you have information to share.
- Be prepared. Present information concisely, using nonlibrary terminology.
- Listen carefully both to what is said and to what is not said.
- Leave information in printed format for later analysis and reflection.

For regularly scheduled meetings such as board meetings, you may be expected to prepare the agenda, integrating matters board members wish to discuss with matters you need to have discussed.

ACTION TWO: Provide administration with detailed information about needs.

- Describe how the need was determined.
- List the activities needed to alleviate the need.
- Provide accurate information concerning personnel and budget implications.
- Cite ways to determine success if activities are implemented.

ACTION THREE: Make administrators look good.

- Provide information about successful projects.
- Collect affirmative reactions from users.

- Share applause you receive.

- Represent your library as a successful operation at as many outside events as possible.

- Develop audiovisual records of events that your administrator can share with colleagues.

ACTION FOUR: Meet with other departments.

- Share concerns and probable outcomes.

- Discuss problems and solutions, theirs as well as yours.

- Offer to help them.

- Suggest projects that will be mutually beneficial.

New Kids on the Block

Changes in management may occur. Persons who outline expectations for your performance may themselves change positions, retire, or leave the organization. When administrators leave, you may want to review the reasons for those departures. In the political arena, an election may be responsible for new leadership, and you should review the platform of the newly elected officials. If an official's platform included a reduction in costs of operations, you should immediately review your library budget, because all budgets will become candidates for close scrutiny. Planning justifications for budget items will prepare you when cuts are suggested.

Thus, when new administrators become responsible for the operation of the library,

- research the likes and dislikes of the new administrators related to their information needs;

- listen to what they are saying and not saying;

- analyze how to make them look good;

- determine what you may do to help them with their assignments; and

- become an important member of their team.

When officers retire, those promoted to replace the retirees must be made aware of the importance of the library in the lives of patrons. New administrators have new agendas, and it is important that you and your library become important to them.

In conclusion, staff in the library have been hired and trained. It is now time for you to learn the procedures that allow the library to open. As previously stated, most persons believe that libraries exist to circulate materials and equipment. The next chapter describes how to circulate the holdings of the library to patrons.

Chapter 4

CIRCULATION OF MATERIALS AND EQUIPMENT

Libraries exist to provide information for their patrons. Materials circulate to allow the user easy access to needed information, to allow users to take the material to a location away from the library, and to permit use of that information for the time required by the user. You will work constantly to make finding and using materials an easy process. This concern for ease of access is reflected in rules and regulations that encourage rather than discourage frequent visits to the library. Artificial barriers, and most barriers are artificial, may make visiting the library a problem rather than a solution, an unpleasant rather than a pleasant happening. If you and your staff are to project an image of information providers who are helping people rather than keeping the collection, then access, use, and circulation of the collection must be made simple. When the effort to use the library is greater than any effects of not having the information, few will come to your library.

CIRCULATION DECISIONS

Your most obvious activity is checking out materials. Remembering who borrowed a copy of a book from our home or office library is only slightly more difficult than remembering where we last saw it. Keeping accurate records of who has items from the library, when they are expected to be returned so that the next user can gain custody, and crediting the person who returns the materials with having done so is important. Otherwise, most libraries would be decimated by users in a short time. Such record keeping must be well organized, so that records of circulating materials are easily verified and users can be rapidly located if someone else needs the material.

When a library has been in existence for a long time, the decisions will have been made and the actual processes will be in place. You may wish to see if the methods used are successful or if some changes need to be made.

If the library is new, decisions are necessary, including how to identify each item and each borrower, how long materials should circulate, and what must be done if materials are not returned on time.

DECISION ONE: How to identify individual items.

Each item must have an identifier that is unique to it to confirm exactly which of two identical items is checked out by a borrower, sent on interlibrary loan, away at the bindery, lost, or discarded. When an item is returned, this identifier confirms that this was the exact item checked out. You must determine which one or what combination of the following to use as identifiers: author's name, title, call number, accession number, copy number, or bar code. Once the decision is made, the information will be placed on records used in the circulation process.

ACTION ONE: Assign copy numbers.

In assigning copy numbers, take care that you know exactly how many copies of an item you own, so that you do not assign "copy 2" to three items when, in fact, you have copy 2, copy 3, and copy 4.

Example of an identifier with author, title, call number, and copy number: For: Sutton, (and) So You're Going to Run a Library, (and) Z675 S3W873 (and) copy 1.

ALTERNATIVE ACTION ONE: Assign accession numbers.

In bygone days, accession numbers were assigned from an accession book. Information about each item was placed there, so that replacements could be made if items were lost. Author, title, publisher, date, vendor, full price, discounted price, and other miscellaneous information were kept. The accession book and the shelflist were the record of the library's holdings in case of fire. Much of this information quickly becomes inaccurate: prices go up, books go out of print, and vendors go out of business. Accession books quickly become obsolete because the information there is incorrect. However, you may wish to assign consecutive numbers to items as identifiers, merely recording the last number you assigned.

Example: For: Sutton, (and) So You're Going to Run a Library, (and) 16,202 [accession number].

ALTERNATIVE ACTION TWO: Assign bar codes.

Fig. 4.1. Example of a bar code.

Bar codes are placed on items when there is an automated circulation system. Bar codes may be ordered from suppliers, or they may be supplied as a part of the system you purchase. Some computer programs will generate bar codes for you.

Items are given unique identifiers most often when they are processed. How and why these are assigned will be discussed in more depth in chapter 7. Unique identifiers help you confirm exactly which item is checked out by the borrower and if the one returned is the same item checked to the patron. Who has borrowed an item is also of special importance. When a request for that item is made by another patron the item should be recalled.

Most patrons appreciate knowing when they might expect to receive the item they have requested. If materials cannot be recalled, it may indicate a need to try to find the item or similar materials for the patron in another library. The length of time items circulate affects your ability to provide items to users.

DECISION TWO: How long should items circulate?

Not all items may circulate the same length of time, depending on category or format. Also, some formats will circulate differently to each category of user. Lengths of time:

- Days (one, two, three, four, five)

- Weeks (one, two, three, four, five)

- Months (one, two, three, four, five)

- Longer (one semester, one year)

- Indefinitely

ACTION ONE: Choose length of time.

The traditional length of time for checkout of most items in most libraries has been two weeks, but this is traditional rather than realistic in many situations, and it is certainly not a law. Different lengths of time apply for different formats or types of materials. Reserve and reference materials might have only overnight use because they are needed in the library when it is open. Some more popular fiction in limited supply may have a seven-day checkout to accommodate more users. Special formats such as videotapes or 16mm films may circulate for less than a week. Few collections will have only one format of materials, and decisions must be made for each.

When you have a wide variety of materials in many formats, including print (books, pamphlets, research reports, and magazines on paper and microfiche) and nonprint (films, videos, filmstrips, tape recordings, slides, pictures), the length of time needed for use may vary by format. A videotape may be viewed in total in two hours; whereas it may take a great deal longer to read a book or take the notes needed from magazine articles. A patron may wish to borrow slides to prepare a presentation three weeks in the future, although the actual showing is only 45 minutes. Record in your manual the circulation period for each format, as in the example shown in figure 4.2.

```
Formats of materials:
    books: 3 weeks
    magazines: 3 weeks
    films or videotapes: 2 days
    records or tapes: 1 week
    pictures or slides: 1 week
    vertical file: 2 weeks
    and so on
```

Fig. 4.2. Circulation periods for various formats.

Please note that having a variety of circulation times may be confusing to volunteers. Further, if circulation is not automated, you will need several date-due stamps. With automation, you must program your system to recognize each item with its separate circulation period.

ACTION TWO: Identify special users.

Categories or characteristics of users may also dictate the length of time an item may be borrowed. In an elementary school, students who come to the library every week may need only one week's circulation period because books are shorter and students read them quickly. In a high school or public library, a longer time might be needed when materials circulating could take a longer time to complete use. In the case of corporations or agencies, users may need materials for a long time, and one user may be the only person really interested in the item. This is discussed further in this chapter beginning on page 49.

Categories of Users:

- Students

- Teachers

- Residents (adult collection; children's room)

- Employees

- Congregation (clergy, teachers, members)

ACTION THREE: Consider circulation limits.

You should give careful thought before limiting circulation. You create bad public relations when use is restricted to one group or when any user is denied access to any part of the library collection. When one user is allowed a longer circulation period than another, your decision may be challenged. When one category of user, e.g., students, may keep an item for only two weeks, they may question why their teachers may hold an item indefinitely. Children who are not allowed in the adult collection when they are young may have a poorer perception of library services when they become voting adults.

As mentioned earlier, it may also be difficult to maintain accurate records when materials circulate for different lengths of time or not at all, and for different lengths of time for some library users. This especially poses problems when you must explain circulation procedures to staff and volunteers, some or all of whom may work at the circulation desk irregularly. It may also slow down checkout when a different date-due stamp is needed for each of several formats, or if some items must have dates entered manually.

DECISION THREE: *How will users be identified?*

As shown in the examples below, users may sign their books out by writing their name on a book card. They may be required to bring a borrower's card each time they come to the library, with a bar code or some other machine identifier. Or, you may maintain a bar code file in a box, in a drawer, or on a Rolodex. Your decision will be based on how you maintain careful borrower records. This will be discussed later in the chapter.

signature

3 1735 029 423 856

3 1735 029 423 898

Die Number: H102

bar code

Denver Public Library

membership card

DECISION FOUR: *How and where to keep records?*

Information concerning which users have what materials and equipment should be kept near where materials are checked out and returned, usually close to the entrance to the library. This makes it easy for you to acknowledge return of items and allows another borrower immediate access to the material.

How:

- Book cards with date-due slips
- Borrower cards
- Machine-readable record
- Notebook near items
- Some of the above
- All of the above

Where:

- Circulation desk
- Computer

Records are kept at the chargeout desk where patrons check out and return materials. These are kept in a file so that cards will not be lost or in a machine-readable database that you must back up (make a floppy disk record of what is on the computer) each day at the close of circulation. This will be discussed in more depth later in this chapter when discussing how to minimize overdue materials.

DECISION FIVE: How to handle overdue items?

What will you do about items that are not returned by the due date? When many patrons are anxious to borrow the same item and only one copy is available, it becomes essential that materials be returned as soon as possible. Materials are requested after book talks have been given, when an assignment is made, when a new movie is produced, when best-seller lists are published, or after many other public relations events. All of these events make items desirable to many users, and efforts are needed to see that materials are returned as soon as possible, on or immediately after the date due. When patrons are delinquent, you must choose a method to remind them that they have an item that is overdue. The following are some methods to use:

Overdue notices

- Hand-delivered
- Mailed

Personal contacts

- Notification of teacher, parent, or administrator
- Limited checkout for next library visit

DECISION SIX: How to enforce rules?

Choosing a penalty is always difficult. Fines and restriction of library privileges are two common types of penalties. You must make a careful judgment between what is fair and acceptable to patrons and what will encourage patrons to steal or mutilate rather than borrow information. This is discussed again in the section in this chapter on monitoring delinquent borrowers.

When you have identified all your procedures, post the rules and regulations where they can be seen by all. You may wish to prepare a handout to give to all first-time users.

Reference Books

Users may expect some materials, such as reference books, to be available at all times in the library. Certainly few persons read a reference book from cover to cover. When there is only one set of encyclopedias, and the set is in constant use throughout the day, you may be reluctant to let a single volume be taken away for even a short time.

It is the belief of this author that everything should circulate from most libraries. Allowing total access to the collection lessens the tendency for those who need information to mutilate materials by taking one or more pages away from the library. Because few libraries are open 24 hours a day, reference books can circulate overnight, if not for short times during the day. If reference materials are limited to use in libraries, you may be asked to differentiate between references needed for short-answer questions, such as the *Guinness Book of World Records,* and those reference tools such as *Granger's Index to Poetry* that refer the patron to a book in the library. It would be difficult to explain why *Granger* should remain on the shelf when the library is closed and even more difficult to justify locking up the *Book of World Records.*

When Equipment Is Needed

Depending on format, information may require equipment for access. Users who take a novel home to read need no additional equipment except lighting after dark. A videotape for their child's birthday party requires a videotape player, an item rapidly becoming standard to most, but not all, households. However, 16mm films, filmstrips, microcomputer software, and microfiche require projectors, computers, and readers not often found in homes. When patrons do not have the necessary equipment at home, these formats are limited to use in the library, or equipment is made available to borrow for use outside the library.

Equipment may circulate from the library. A carrying case is provided to protect the equipment as it moves in and out of buildings and vehicles. Extra bulbs, extension cords, adapters, and screens are all packed, so that the user will have the necessary accessories when using the items. Lightweight filmstrip and microfiche viewers are available. The rapidly decreasing cost of laptop computers may make them a more realistic item to lend. As more films are produced in videotape format and more homes have VCRs, this problem may also be alleviated.

Use of materials is limited to the library when, as noted above, accompanying equipment is not available off-site. Such use requires special considerations for you. Because materials are both audio and visual, an enclosed area is needed to cut the distraction of sound and motion from other library users.

ACCESS TO USERS

Providing access to users means analyzing who expects to take advantage of your library.

DECISION SEVEN: Who are your actual users?

Who is allowed to borrow materials is another decision point. You should be willing to check out any item in the library to any user who has a need for materials and wishes to borrow them from that library. Through interlibrary loan requests, items may be sent to any state within the United States, and some may be requested from and sent to foreign countries. Conversely, you may be asked to limit your actual users to some population within the agency or within an area.

Some distinctions may be made between long-term and short-term users. Some patrons may be frequent visitors to the library, checking out and returning materials in a limited time. Others may wish to keep materials for a much longer time. As discussed earlier under circulation limits, teachers and researchers may require materials for longer use; therefore, they may need to circulate items beyond the established circulation period, subject to recall if needed by someone else. You must also consider if any parts of your collection are closed to any group within your potential clientele.

DECISION EIGHT: Whether to close any collection areas.

Many reasons can be found for closing some areas of the collection to some groups. Some might suggest situations where it is appropriate to place limits, such as those based on age discrimination. That is, in a school library, elementary students may not be allowed to take materials from the high school collection, or children may not be allowed to use the adult collection in the public library. If you are a school librarian, you may think it necessary to limit the collection to students attending the school and even to question parent use of the library's materials.

Before limiting any user's access to any part of any materials collection, consider carefully your need to do so and the consequences of depriving any user of information that might be gained from full use of a collection. Age discrimination is seldom valid; children are studying topics at an earlier age and in more depth than most present-day adults had an opportunity to do in their early education. Further, students often cover a topic briefly in the classrooms and wish to continue independent research in more depth while their classmates move into a new area of study. The very premise of the gifted programs is to permit students to expand their horizons, and this concept should not be limited to one group of students. As far as parents using materials, they are the taxpayers who purchased the materials in the first place. Most parents who come into a school library do so to find materials to use with their children at home; to limit their use is to deprive them of the ability to help and even learn with their children.

Limiting public school collections from use by private school students is also questionable. The parents of these students pay taxes to the school district as well as tuition for a private school for their children. Were they not paying the tuition, their children would be students in the public schools.

As the home school movement widens, public school collections will continue to be open to these children and their parents. Wider access to library collections will expand opportunities for children to locate the information they need. Serious consideration must be given when barriers to information are created by restricting access to materials.

Another restriction is limiting use of materials to persons within a governmental area such as a public library jurisdiction. Legal boundaries of school districts do not necessarily coincide with boundaries of public library districts; thus, some students attending a school may not be able to use the same public library as their peers. Again, such barriers deprive students of needed resources, and school and public librarians can work together to minimize such limitations. Barriers and limitations are rapidly disappearing through shared resources, statewide library cards, and other cooperative ventures. In this case a little cooperation will go a long way toward building a more literate society.

The age of interlibrary loan has arrived. Interlibrary loan services have widened access to collections in all types of libraries for all users. Most often materials are loaned to a borrower who "belongs" to a public library service area, school, or corporation. At other times, patrons may be affiliated with a neighboring public library, school, or corporation. Statewide library cards open use of materials in public libraries to anyone who is registered in a "home" library. Networks and consortiums, delivery systems, CD-ROM and microfiche databases of library holdings, and online bibliographic databases have created access to shared resources for interlibrary loan and cooperative purchase. It is likely that this activity will increase as more libraries have their holdings on databases.

RECORDING CIRCULATION

Careful records are maintained for the circulation of materials. The place where materials circulate may help determine the method of recording the transaction and tracing the return of the item.

DECISION NINE: To maintain careful records.

How materials are circulated depends on where materials circulate, or the location of the circulation desk, type of patron identification required, and whether there are manual or automated circulation systems. Circulation of materials can be most efficiently handled in a small library from a single location identified as the chargeout desk. This is where the exchange of items takes place, where the borrower checks out the item, and where the records of what is checked out of the library remain.

Manual Systems

When a manual system is in use, you place card and pocket on items so they can be checked out. This card and pocket have the name of the item and the author when there is an author. If there is more than one copy of the item, this is indicated using one of the methods chosen under "Decision One: How to identify individual items" on page 43. In this way, a user returning one copy of an item will be credited with its return, while a user with a second copy of the same item still has that one.

You may use a larger card for magazines, with the name of the magazine at the top. The date or volume number is recorded as each single magazine is checked out. Slips of paper or cards may be used to record materials taken from the vertical file or from the audiovisual materials collection.

Another method is to record materials on the actual borrower's card or record. That is, a record of what is checked out is kept by the borrower's name, rather than cards for individual items recording the borrower's name. In many school districts where automated circulation systems have not yet been installed in school libraries, children place book cards in classroom files or in poster sheets with pockets labeled with each child's name. Students can file their checkout information in their individual pockets and return the cards to the items when they return the items. In a small library with only special formats such as all microfiche or mostly periodical literature or only a few patrons, maintaining a borrower's record may be easier than devising a more elaborate system. It would be especially true if you were collecting information and forwarding it to the patron rather than having the patron come to the library.

With manual systems, the chargeout desk will have containers for circulation cards. The containers may be wooden trays manufactured for a library chargeout desk or they may be some locally created card holder, such as a shoe box.

When wooden trays are available, you will choose whether to place the cards for materials checked out behind the date the materials are to be returned, or to place cards by the classroom or department of the borrower. Within the designated area, you will decide whether to place the cards in alphabetical order by the author's last name or in their sequence as if they were on the library shelves. That is, fiction items are in alphabetical order by author, and nonfiction are in their numerical sequence. For items without individual checkout cards, such as magazines or documents, a larger card may be stored in another file.

Automated Systems

Automated systems vary with the complexity of the system chosen. Most automated systems use a bar code that has been placed on each item in the collection, confirming its unique identification. A light pen is then used to check out the materials, and a computer printout is created of each day's circulation. Such a system requires a companion bar code to identify the users. As discussed earlier in the chapter under circulation decisions:

- You may choose to issue a borrower's card with bar code and make it the patrons' responsibility to keep their cards.

- You may prefer to keep borrowers' cards in the library rather than release them to their owners. Use of file boxes or a Rolodex is suggested for maintaining borrowers' bar codes in the library, although this will be very slow when you have many borrowers hoping to check out materials at a particular time.

Whatever system is used, you need to know who has which items from the collection and the date the material is to be returned. In schools, administrators need records to clear students who are changing schools. Public librarians must answer requests from families who are moving out of town and want to know what items they have checked out. When materials are checked out for an indefinite period, you must be able to find out where items are, so you can recall them for use by other patrons.

Materials are returned to the library on or before the date due. Care must be taken to give credit to the borrower for returning the material. This borrower's bar code must be read with the item being returned; or, when a pocket and card are attached to the item, the correct book card is returned to the pocket. If a fine is charged for overdue materials, a record is made that the fine was paid or not paid.

CONFIDENTIALITY OF RECORDS

Confidentiality of information about any borrower's record has become a legal obligation in some states. Laws prohibit the identification of users of any items in the library; therefore, you may be required to keep the circulation of materials confidential.

DECISION TEN: To retain borrower's confidentiality.

Automated circulation systems are the easiest method to accomplish this. Otherwise, you must devise a method of obliterating the name of the user when the material is returned. To do this manually, a system of dual cards can be used. The user signs a blank card and this is attached to the actual card. When the material is returned, the actual card is returned to the item and the blank card is placed with other cards to be signed by the next users. Another method is to use the system described above, where users place the borrower's cards in envelopes with their names on them or in a section of the charging tray with their department affiliation.

Obviously, retaining confidentiality means that you and your staff must refuse to divulge the names of patrons in relationship to the materials they are using. This may be difficult to do, depending on who is asking. Parents will assume they have the right to know what their children are reading. Teachers may question you under the guise that they need to know if students are reading the assigned materials. Public librarians have even been approached by FBI agents. To report circulation of materials to anyone is at best gossip and at worst illegal.

DELINQUENT BORROWERS

In the best of all possible worlds, every user would return every borrowed item on or before the date due. Such a world will never exist, and it is inevitable that you will have delinquent borrowers.

DECISION ELEVEN: Monitor delinquent borrowers.

Keeping materials beyond the allocated loan period may seem to be the rule rather than the exception. A shorter circulation period will usually generate a larger number of overdue items. Because sending notices to users can become a real burden when you are responsible for so many other tasks in the library, a more flexible policy allowing a longer circulation time relieves you of some of this drudgery. The caveat that materials may be called back from the borrower if another person requests them alleviates concern that materials will not be available when needed.

If you have a patron who regularly violates circulation rules, you will need to discuss this to see if you can, together, determine why this happens and decide what measures should be taken to improve the situation.

ACTION ONE: Minimizing overdue materials.

After identifying the length of time for materials to circulate, deciding how to record circulation, and noting the delinquent borrowers, you must decide how to recall items that are overdue or requested by another patron. Choose a consistent method to cover this situation.

When materials are not returned on time, you may notify borrowers in the following ways:

- Send overdue notes to borrowers, requesting that items be returned as soon as possible. These can be hand-delivered, mailed to borrowers, mailed to parents or employers.

- Send second, third, and fourth notices after additional waiting periods.

When circulation periods are longer than the traditional two weeks or indefinite, or when someone requests an item that is in circulation, send a note to the borrower, asking that the item be returned as soon as possible. Consider purchasing second copies of often recalled items.

ACTION TWO: Determine penalties.

- Assess a fine.

You may wish to assess a fine when an item is not returned on time. This assessment for forgetting or neglecting to return materials is, in the consideration of this author, the worst of all possible public relations policies for any library. Justified by some as a way to "teach responsibility," this concept has never been proven to make patrons more responsible. It has yet to be shown how assessing this fee teaches consideration of others, and it often encourages those who fear they might forget to return something to rip out pages rather than check out an entire document.

Users who are able to pay their fines keep the materials as long as they wish and pay as a matter of course. Payment seems to alleviate the need to bring the material back. After all, they are, in a sense, "renting" the item. Fines may inhibit the use of materials by others who cannot afford to pay and are reluctant to check out materials in case they should be unable to return them on time.

- Withdraw borrowing privileges.

When materials are not returned on time, a popular punishment is to withdraw further borrowing privileges from the patron. Again, the author is reluctant to suggest that such limitations be placed. Reports in library literature where individuals have been caught with thousands of books taken illegally from many libraries prove that it is possible to take materials without charging them. This punishment might teach how to steal rather than teach responsibility. It also seems wasteful to tell six-year-olds that they cannot take another book until they remember to return the one they have. Would it not be better to take an affirmative position and reward and applaud those who remember to return their materials? Perhaps you should post a lesson over the circulation desk that reads:

Do unto others as you would have others do unto you!

Consideration for other patrons is a more positive lesson to teach than sending the sheriff to a home. Discussing the situation privately with repeat offenders may help identify their problem and help them solve it. This will benefit everyone.

COUNTING CIRCULATION

A circulation count, or record of use, is sometimes needed to explain the importance of the collection both inside and outside the library. This means that an attempt is made to keep a record of the use of materials. It can be done in the following ways:

- You may actually count the number of items checked out each day.

- You may make this count on random days of the month and use that as an average count.

- If you have an automated circulation system, maintaining records of circulation is greatly simplified.

Counting circulation is useful for showing the need for increased funds to add materials to the collection. However, a circulation count shows only what materials were taken from the shelves, not the actual use of any item. It is impossible to determine if the item has served the need of the borrower unless the borrower is queried about each item as it is returned.

WHEN FEES ARE CHARGED

Librarians have been considering free versus fee services in libraries for some time. Early public libraries in the United States were subscription libraries, open only to those who could afford the membership fee to use the materials. The public library movement changed this concept to provide free access to information for all citizens, and public librarians continue to offer materials to their clientele free of charge. Discussion of the perceived need to charge for more costly services follows; however, the policy of charging fees must be carefully analyzed. If, by charging a fee, a library restricts any patron from access to information, fees should not be assessed. Users need information. Keeping information from them because they cannot afford to buy it is inexcusable.

Some public schools provide free textbooks; others make a rental charge. Use of materials in school libraries is free, and anyone working in a school should consider carefully the charge of fines for overdue books, because this may be perceived by both parents and students as a fee for service. It may also encourage parents to refuse to let their children take materials from the library. Charging for the use of materials in the public library can also severely limit access to information.

DECISION TWELVE: Fee or free?

Despite your protests, the governing board of your library may dictate that costs be charged back to the user. In special libraries, this may be to the department within the company in which the employee making the request works. In public and school libraries, costs will most often be charged directly to the person making the request. You may be told what items will have fees assessed and how much, or you may be asked for your suggestions.

ACTION ONE: When use of items is fee-based.

Deciding which services to assess and what to charge can be based on your perception of those services that are acceptable for charging your patrons.

- Best-sellers

One charge is sometimes made for special materials such as best-selling novels. This fee is for the use of the book for a limited period, usually seven days. The theory is that the person who really wants to read the best-seller immediately will be willing to pay, thereby generating income to purchase more best-sellers or other materials. Persons who do not want to pay to read the book can wait until it is taken from the seven-day shelf, when it will be available free of charge.

- Copy machines

Some libraries have coin-operated copy machines for patron use, and in some libraries, this is a profit-making activity. In fact, in some communities the library is a most accessible location for a copy machine, rivaled only by the post office. Copy capability is useful, and many patrons are pleased with a location to copy tax returns and other personal items. However, this becomes an added cost to the library user who must copy information when it is unavailable for checkout.

Persons may not expect to make free copies of library materials for their own use. However, if library materials are being mutilated because of restrictive copying charges, you may consider offering limited copying at no charge. When the cost charged covers only the actual costs of the copy machine to the library, it seems less punitive than other types of charges.

- Online searching

Online searching fees are charged in many libraries. However, this can severely limit access to information for those who cannot pay and may more quickly divide the world into the information haves and have-nots.

- Videotapes

Fees may be suggested for videotapes used outside the library. You may want to consider the viewpoint of the local video rental store owner, a taxpayer, who may consider the library in competition. The librarian must also weigh the perceptions of the public at large, including the poor public relations such a charge may generate.

- Microcomputer use

Coin boxes attached to a timed use of microcomputers have also been seen as revenue-generating activities in the library. In some libraries, this is perceived as the only possible way to pay for microcomputers for patron use. Such charges exacerbate the distance between users who have resources and those who do not.

In deciding to charge fees for materials, please consider the following:

- Which patrons will be denied access because fees are charged?

- Where do the fees go?

- Will fees increase the mutilation of materials?

- Will fees cause negative public relations?

- Is any alternative available?

- What will opening the door to charges for service signal to

  the community?
  the staff?
  the administration?
  the funding officials?

ACTION TWO: Determine how much to charge.

Most libraries and information centers are not in business to make money. To keep patrons supportive of your library, consider charging only what the service costs you, and let them know what that charge is. As mentioned earlier in discussing copy machines, online searching, and microcomputers, you should not be widening the chasm between the information haves and the have-nots.

ACTION THREE: Keep careful records.

- Patrons are charged only for their use of any fee-based service.

- Records are kept to see the actual income in relation to any loss of clientele, and so on.

It may be that the clerical time involved and the loss of favorable public relations that comes from charging fees may make charging fees a loss rather than a profit. Suggestions for assessing the cost accountability of fees are given in chapter 8.

COPYRIGHT

Copy machines in libraries offer alternatives to checking out print materials. The patron can make a copy of the information rather than carry the material away from the library. You must be aware of copyright regulations and see that all library users observe copyright in their copying of materials.

The Association of American Publishers has joined with the National Association of College Stores, Inc., to publish a pamphlet titled, "Questions and Answers on Copyright for the Campus Community." The booklet is available from the National Association of College Stores, Inc., 528 E. Lorain St., Oberlin, OH, 44074-1298. Because permission is granted to reproduce the booklet or any part of its contents, the following is quoted from page 1:

> Reproduction of copyrighted material without prior permission of the copyright owner, particularly in an educational setting, is an issue of concern for the academic community. Unfortunately, the impropriety of much unauthorized copying is all too often overlooked by users in an educational setting.
>
> Although copying all or a part of a work without obtaining permission may appear to be an easy and convenient solution to an immediate problem, such unauthorized copying can frequently violate the rights of the author or publisher of the copyrighted work, and be directly contrary to the academic mission to teach respect for ideas and for the intellectual property which expresses those ideas.
>
> Without understanding the copyright law, including elements such as the doctrine of "Fair Use" and its application and limitations in the educational setting, faculty members, copy centers, college stores, universities and colleges themselves, and others, will be at risk for engaging in illegal photocopying.

On page 3 of this pamphlet are described the types of works that hold copyright protection:

> "[O]riginal works of authorship" which are "fixed in a tangible medium of expression." Among the types of works which are subject to copyright protection are literary, dramatic, musical, choreographic and pictorial works, graphic works, pantomimes, sound recordings, sculptures, motion pictures and audio-visual works. These categories include fact works (including dictionaries and directories), video cassettes and computer programs and databases.

Copyright protection does not include ideas, procedures, processes, systems, concepts, principles or discoveries, although these may be protectable under patent or trade secret laws. However, literary or other forms of expression of these ideas (and the like) is covered by copyright.

You will become aware of copyright regulations and adhere to them. You should encourage all other information users to obey copyright. Sometimes situations make it difficult to enforce this, but copyright is the law. If you do not honor copyright rules, it will be difficult for you to expect users to obey library rules.

Methods of circulating materials have been discussed. In the chapter that follows, the role of reference service is outlined.

GLOSSARY

Shelflist. A card file arranged as the library is arranged. That is, in Dewey or LC numbers, and used to take an inventory of the collection. As libraries become machine-readable with online public access systems, these become records on disk read by bar code.

Chapter 5

REFERENCE IN THE LIBRARY

Simply stated, reference is referring users to information they need. This may be the actual answer, an item that contains the answer, or an agreement to help locate information by telephone, E-mail, fax, or any other means. If your patron has a question about Indiana, you may be able to satisfy that request by finding a picture of the governor in a magazine or an entire book on the history of Indiana, or you may need to call another library to find out the number of museums in the state. Most users will not care where you locate the answer, but they will care if you do not, and they may quickly become anti-library. Another important responsibility is to find the correct answer. If you do not carefully check information, they may learn later that the answer was incorrect, and this will detract from your good image in the community.

Your reference services are considered successful if the user receives the correct information in a timely fashion. This chapter will help you plan successful reference services. It covers reference sources that may be found in your library, beginning steps in locating reference information, and suggestions for determining what users really want to know.

Four kinds of reference situations you might encounter include the following:

- Locating information

- Ready reference questions

- Reference searches for more detailed information

- Expanded reference searches for in-depth researchers

The first, locating information, will be a simple question—"Where are your mystery books?"—with a quick answer. You only need to point out the shelves with mystery books. "Ready reference" is finding a quick answer in the card catalog, a reference book, or other information source. If a patron asks, "Who wrote *Murder on the Orient Express*?" you could locate the answer in the card catalog (if you own the book) or in *Books in Print* (if the item is a book and is still in print). You might be aware that this book was written by Agatha Christie, but you should make sure. Sometimes there are two items with the same title. A response from your personal storehouse of knowledge should be prefaced with, "I believe that answer is 'X,' but let's check it."

Reference searches result from a more in-depth need for detailed information and require a great deal more looking through many reference books, online searches, and your entire collection. You will want to find all you can about the requested topic. The term "expanded reference" describes meeting in-depth research needs. This often means going outside your library to secure items from other locations. The bottom line is to help users find the information they need.

You are better able to help users when you are familiar with information in your library collection. For this reason, a corporation executive could consider the heaviest user of documents as the logical person to organize them for access by others. If you are not yet acquainted with basic references and resources available in your own library, beginning with the mechanics of searching for information and some basic types of reference sources, you may find the following steps helpful:

- Check card catalog or online public access catalog.

- Provide encyclopedia.

- Look in ready reference sources.

- Check an annotated bibliography of reference works to locate a possible source of additional information.

While you are checking the card catalog, ready reference sources, or an annotated bibliography of reference works, you may help your user begin research with an encyclopedia. If an adult public library user wants very basic information about a subject, a nonfiction book on the topic from the children's or young adult collection might help. This will provide a background for patrons and prepare them for more in-depth explanations.

USING THE CARD CATALOG

A manual search through the card catalog or an automated search through the online public access catalog is usually the first step for you and your users in seeking information in your library. Teaching children card catalog skills has been the objective of library instruction from elementary school through bibliographic instruction in graduate school. If you need a brief refresher course, the card catalog or online public access catalog is accessed through three basic search queries: author, title, or subject heading. Additional information may be given in an annotation, or additional subject headings may be listed on this record. When your catalog is automated, another line on the record may tell you if the item is available in the library, or, if checked out, when it will be returned.

The various cards in the card catalog are named for the item on the first line of each card. Examples of the three basic types, author, title, and subject, are shown in figures 5.1, 5.2, and 5.3 on pages 61-62.

Author Card

As shown in figure 5.1, authors are identified by last names, and cards are filed with the last name first. Although some items may have more than one author, and additional cards for joint authors may be found, it is the first author who is used for *main entry*.

```
Z675      Sutton, David
S3W873       So you're going to run a library : A
          library management primer / David Sutton.
          -- Englewood, Colo. : Libraries Unlimited,
          1995.
             xii, 181p. : ill. ; 28 cm.

             Includes bibliographies and index.

             1. Library administration.  2. Media
          programs (education) -- Management.
          3. Public libraries.  4. School libraries
          -- Administration.  I. Title.
```

Fig. 5.1. An author card, which is the main entry card.

Title Card

Title cards begin with the title of the book on the first line. They are filed in alphabetical order by the first word of the title, with the exception of titles beginning with "a" "an," or "the." To find the title in a card catalog, searchers must have a correct title, if that is the only information they have about the item.

```
             So you're going to run a library
Z675      Sutton, David
S3W873       So you're going to run a library : A
          library management primer / David Sutton.
          -- Englewood, Colo. : Libraries Unlimited,
          1995.
             xii, 181p. : ill. ; 28 cm.

             Includes bibliographies and index.

             1. Library administration.  2. Media
          programs (education) -- Management.
          3. Public libraries.  4. School libraries
          -- Administration.  I. Title.
```

Fig. 5.2. A sample title card.

Subject Card

As discussed in chapter 1, materials may have information on several subjects. Subject headings describe topics that are included in each item. When books, filmstrips, or other materials cover more than one topic, each subject heading assigned will have a separate subject card in the card catalog. Subject headings assigned are included on the bottom of each of the catalog cards, so that they may become suggested headings for further research if the citation you have located does not have what you need. The subject card for the first subject listed on the main entry and title card for *So You're Going to Run a Library* is shown in figure 5.3.

```
            LIBRARY ADMINISTRATION
Z675    Sutton, David
S3W873      So you're going to run a library : A
        library management primer / David Sutton.
        -- Englewood, Colo. : Libraries Unlimited,
        1995.
            xii, 181p. : ill. ; 28 cm.

        Includes bibliographies and index.

            1. Library administration.  2. Media
        programs (education) -- Management.
        3. Public libraries.  4. School libraries
        -- Administration.  I. Title.
```

Fig. 5.3. Sample subject card.

As discussed in chapter 1, discovering the word or words used for subject headings may be difficult if you are not accustomed to library cataloging and classification. Subject headings are usually provided through a published list such as Library of Congress or *Sears List of Subject Headings*, but these may not correspond to the patron's first choice of a search strategy. That is, the patron may look up "kittens" when, as shown below, one subject heading list identifies this topic as "CATS" and another list might call it "FELINES." Catalogs should contain cross-references to alternate words, but no card catalog and few databases could provide every possible synonym that a patron might choose.

<table>
<tr><td>CATS.</td><td>FELINES.</td></tr>
<tr><td>Smith, John</td><td>Smith, John</td></tr>
<tr><td>My book about cats.</td><td>My book about cats.</td></tr>
</table>

If your library uses a thesaurus of terms from a database in heavy use, and if the terms in the subject heading list for the remainder of the collection are different, you may wish to make cross-references from the terms most often used to locate information from the database. (See discussion in chapter 1 on choosing subject headings or refer to a book on this topic.)

A wise organizer of information chooses one list and does cross-references from alternative terms back to the basic terms, rather than creating synonymous terms to describe items added to the collection. Cross-references to a chosen term help users find the exact subject; this is preferable to expecting them to locate several synonymous terms to describe the same topic.

WHAT FILING SYSTEM DO YOU USE?

Two filing systems, alphabetical order and word by word, are commonly used. Once a librarian new to a library asked the clerk, "What filing system do you use?" The clerk's puzzled response, "What do you mean, 'filing system'?" told the librarian exactly why it was so difficult to find anything in the card catalog. Books describing filing systems are cited in the annotated bibliography (page 171).

The decision on the type of filing system will have been made in an existing library, but it is a decision point for a new library.

DECISION ONE: Which filing system?

Although different rules exist within filing systems, the major difference between the two basic filing systems is that one system looks at each letter in its alphabetical placement, regardless of punctuation or spacing between letters. The other looks at whole words for placement in alphabetical order. The examples that follow may help you decide whether you wish to use word by word or letter by letter.

Word by Word	Letter by Letter
AIR CONDITIONING	AIR CONDITIONING
AIR MAIL SERVICE	AIRCRAFT
AIR PILOTS	AIR MAIL SERVICE
AIR RAID SHELTERS	AIR PILOTS
Air, Thomas	AIRPLANE CARRIERS
AIRCRAFT	AIRPLANES
AIRPLANE CARRIERS	AIR RAID SHELTERS
AIRPLANES	Air, Thomas

A manual such as the *ALA Filing Rules*[1] has both general rules and some special rules. An example includes how to handle actual abbreviations, e.g., Col (Colonel) or Dr. (doctor) that are "arranged exactly as written" or prefixes that are part of the name of persons or places and are filed as if they are spelled out rather than as abbreviations. Again, consistency is needed if your files are to be accessible to patrons. It matters less which filing rules you adopt than that you adopt and follow a prescribed set of filing rules.

LOCATING THE ADDRESS

Once an item has been identified, and the patron wishes to borrow it to use in the library or to take away, the call number or address will help locate the item on the shelves or wherever it is stored. The address for *So You're Going to Run a Library* was Z675 S3W873. Locating the item on the shelf by classification number was shown in chapter 1.

Librarians or patrons must search manually through a card catalog. When an online system is available, searching may be much easier and faster, and access may be possible through words in the title or in an abstract of the item. How these different access points are created is discussed more fully in chapter 7.

Further, when an online catalog is available, a printer may be attached to the terminal, permitting information to be printed from the terminal screen. See figure 5.4 for an example of a printout. This printout indicates if the item is available in the library.

```
Search Request : A=LOERTSCHER              PITTCAT Library Catalog
BOOK - Record 10 of 11 Entries Found                    Long View
-------------------------------------------------------------------------
             TITLE:    Taxonomies of the school library media program
            AUTHOR:    Loertscher, David V., 1940-
         PUBLISHED:    Englewood, Colo. : Libraries Unlimited, 1988.
       DESCRIPTION:    xvi, 336 p. : ill. ; 28 cm.
              ISBN:    0872876624 (soft)
             NOTES:    Includes index.
                       Bibliography: p. 323-330.
SUBJECTS (LIBRARY OF CONGRESS):      (Use s=search)
                       School libraries.
                       Media programs (Education)
ALL SUBJECTS:                            (Use k=<subject>.su.)
                       School libraries.
                       Media programs (Education)
```

Fig. 5.4. Example of online catalog printout. (Duplicated by permission of NOTIS Systems, Inc.)

In the sample cards for *So You're Going to Run a Library*, the call number is found in the left-hand margin. On the screen of an automated system, as shown in figure 5.4, the call number is halfway down the screen.

Figure 5.5 identifies some parts of different call numbers using both LC and Dewey, as well as three letters of the author's last name, Alc for Alcott, and a format designator, FS for filmstrip. Sometimes an item will have no call number on the card catalog record. This usually signals that the item is fiction. In this case, the initials of the author's last name make up that address. Be prepared for the patron who sees no call number and asks you for 398p. The number of pages does not constitute the address for an item.

What does the call number mean?
Z675 — Library of Congress Classification
S3L68 — Cutter number for author

520 — Dewey number
no number or letter — Fiction (filed by author's last name)
Alc — Fiction (filed by author's last name beginning Alc)
FS — format designator

Fig. 5.5.

Items in different formats may also use the call number to signal they are not books and may be shelved in alternate locations. A format indicator such as FS indicates to users that they may need to look in the filmstrip storage cabinet for the item and that equipment may be needed to facilitate use.

If your library does not have a key to the abbreviations and a floor plan identifying the formats and their locations, you should create such a key. An accompanying guide or map explains where items are housed, if not on the regular shelves. Developing such a key and map should help you become more familiar with these alternate materials. Posting your map helps patrons feel comfortable looking for information. Figure 5.6 shows an example of a key.

Keys to Library Holdings
FS — Filmstrips (in cabinet by chargeout desk)
FLM — 16mm Films (behind the chargeout desk, ask at desk)
VF — Vertical Files (in file cabinets in reference section)

Fig. 5.6.

Knowing the contents of your library and items' locations will help you send patrons to the correct answer by the most direct route. This saves time for them and you and decreases frustration levels. The checklist shown in figure 5.7, on page 66, might be helpful in recording your search efforts.

THE SEARCHER'S CHECKLIST

Topic:
Materials located in

_____ book format   _____ periodicals   _____ media
using _____ card/automated catalog _____ online search
If online search, materials found
_____ in library _____ i.l.l. _____ fax _____ E-mail
Reference books queried
_____ encyclopedia
_____ specialized reference books. List:

Approximate time spent on search:
_____ Topic needs more information in library. Materials suggested for purchase:

Fig. 5.7.

DEFINING REFERENCE BOOKS

Reference in the library begins with locating items on the library shelves; however, not all queries require long, detailed answers or responses from several items. Many responses to reference questions are short and may be found in specific books of data that have been collected for quick answers. You will be familiar with dictionaries, thesauri, encyclopedias, and indexes to periodicals. These reference books answer shorter queries. If you must answer many similar questions each day, you will become familiar with references that most often have those answers. You will want them at your fingertips, and you will be reluctant to allow them to circulate, even overnight.

What are reference books? You define them as such by locating them on special shelves. This means you must place a special indicator on the call number to locate it at its special address, and you must decide when to place an item in this section.

Reference books are usually given an "R" or "Ref" at the top of the call number. This indicates their location on the shelf and that they may not circulate for the regular time period.

DECISION TWO: How to decide what is a reference book.

Reference books provide quick answers to brief questions from patrons; they are usually not read cover to cover. However, some reference books will not be as obvious as others. Because items placed in this special collection are defined by the types of questions you must answer, you should begin to analyze your reference questions.

ACTION ONE: Analyze reference questions.

Using the form outlined in figure 5.7, record several days of reference questions and note where you find the answers:

- In an encyclopedia?
- Another reference book? Which one?
- In the regular collection?
- Elsewhere?

If you are frequently locating answers to shorter questions in items on your regular shelves, you may need to move these books to your reference collection.

Another point to consider in answering reference questions is the age of the reference book. When a book has many out-of-date responses, it must be discarded. Further, if a reference book is never used, you need to ask if it simply does not cover any topic of interest to your users or if it is out-of-date. If the answer to either of those questions is yes, then you need to remove that book from the shelves.

Sometimes you get questions that you cannot answer from your collection. If you ask another librarian for help, your request may not be answered until long after the patron has gone. Conversely, it will not take long to wear out your welcome at your friend's library if most of the reference questions being asked are from you. It is then time to think about adding to your reference collection.

ACTION TWO: Decide to add a reference book.

Frequent calls to other librarians to get information from the same reference indicates that you need to add that book or another with similar information to your collection. Adding the item will help you respond to patrons immediately. You might ask the other librarian to tell you which reference books are being used often to answer your queries, so that you can order your own copies.

When a book is purchased that is not readily identified as a reference book, you will decide if it should be given the "Reference" address, limiting its use to the library during regular hours.

DECISION THREE: Determine whether a work is reference or regular collection.

- Should cost of a volume be a factor?

Reference books can be quite costly compared to most other items purchased for the library. Encyclopedias, for example, cost well into the hundreds of dollars and must be updated frequently if the information is to be accurate for the user. It is tempting for some librarians to place very expensive books in the reference section to protect them from theft or loss. Although some reference books may be more expensive, being expensive does not automatically make an item a reference work.

- Does it provide only brief answers?

Materials that provide brief answers to specific questions rather than more extensive information on a topic are usually considered references. Examples are dictionaries that provide brief definitions and pronunciations of words;

encyclopedias with short articles on a wide variety of topics; identification guides to items such as coins, birds, and fish; rule books such as parliamentary procedure or games; indexes to short story collections or poems in poetry books. Books providing statistics about almost anything for which names or numbers can be given, such as *World Almanac* and *Book of Facts,* are also found on the reference shelves. These books, although interesting to a reader, are less likely to be read from cover to cover.

Once the types of reference questions asked have been analyzed, you can begin to decide what books from the regular collection belong in the reference collection and what books in the reference collection are more suitable to the regular collection. For instance, a bird identification book should be in the reference collection, but a patron may wish to take that book or a similar book on a week's camping trip. If this is often the case, purchasing duplicate copies and placing one in each location will help. Children through adults enjoy browsing the *Guinness Book of World Records* and *Famous First Facts.* When sufficient funds allow, these books should be considered for placement in the regular collection as well.

DECISION FOUR: What to add to the collection?

Deciding what to purchase to provide adequate reference information is a difficult selection process. Because most references are costly, you will be reluctant to make an error. Certainly you do not wish to add an expensive book that is never used.

As discussed above, you will select the references that other librarians have been using most often to answer your questions. This will help you give instant responses to patrons and decrease the number of times you must call another library. You will also need to anticipate references that will become useful once you understand them.

Several guides are available for the librarian in the small library, including McCormick's *The New York Times Guide to Reference Materials* and Nichols's *Guide to Reference Books for School Media Centers.* These are described more fully in the annotated bibliography. Also, *Booklist* regularly publishes extensive reviews of forthcoming and recent reference books.

LEARNING TO USE REFERENCE BOOKS
TO ANSWER QUESTIONS

The best way to become familiar with reference books is to use them. If you are unused to locating information in a reference collection, a quick survey of the collection will help. To do this, you should

take a book from the reference shelf.

read the title, preface, introductory pages, and table of contents. These will tell you a little about the book.

read a few of the entries to determine
   a) the amount of information on each topic. Is it one sentence, a paragraph, column, or page?

b) the level of difficulty or depth of information presented. Is it written for an expert or a novice? Will it provide more than a very brief response?

become aware of the arrangement of the information on each page and throughout the reference book. This will help you find answers quicker.

Questions are posed by patrons in the library, over the telephone, or by many other means such as a note carried by a student from the classroom or an "all points" E-mail query. Questions can be short: What is the tallest building in the world? Or they may be somewhat longer: What are the names of the wives of the U.S. presidents? Or very long: Do you have information for a 20-page report on the present-day Civil Rights movement?

Until you become more familiar with your collection, a good start for a reference response is the encyclopedia. While the patron is perusing information there, you can make a more extensive search for additional material. Once you become more familiar with your collection, you will be able to suggest sources more quickly. One newer method for retrieving information is from an online database or reference books or encyclopedias that have been reformatted onto CD-ROM.

THE MIGHTY DATABASE

Early in the development of computers, companies sought ways to increase use of databases they had created for their own purposes; in the process, these companies hoped to profit from their previous work. This was the beginning of online database searching, and this remains a quick method of retrieving information for patrons. It can also be expensive. Retrieval time is one cost, and the cost of output increases with quantity, whether only a brief *citation* or a citation with *abstract* or *full text*. Computerized database searches are usually faster to conduct than manual searches. Also, because new information can be entered much faster than it could be placed in print format and distributed, databases are often more current. A database information retrieval checklist is suggested in figure 5.8.

```
                       DATABASE CHECKLIST
Topic:
Available  ____ online ____number of hits            cost:
           ____ CD-ROM  ____number of hits
Contents:  ____ number of bibliographic citations only
           ____ number of bibliographic citations plus abstract
           ____ number of bibliographic citations plus full text
Number of useful citations ____ printed from computer screen
                           ____ microforms
                           ____ in library's periodicals collection
```

Fig. 5.8.

In the early days of online searching, patrons were usually satisfied with a large number of "hits" and cared less about quality of information. This is no longer the case, and persons searching for answers want relevant sources available to them. Whether searching online databases or online and off-line bibliographic utilities, it is important to help patrons narrow their searches, so that citations found are more likely to be relevant. This reduces the frustration of interlibrary loan librarians who send materials not used by the recipient and users who are overwhelmed by useless information.

FINDING INFORMATION IN NEWSPAPERS AND MAGAZINES

Newspapers and magazines provide up-to-date information regularly for your patrons. Indexes to hundreds of periodicals are currently available to libraries in both print and CD-ROM.

NewsBank Inc. provides CD-ROM index access to articles in more than 600 newspapers on microfiche, and they are presently providing full-text CD-ROM for almost 100 newspapers. This system offers quick access to newspapers, with less than six weeks' delay from publication to shipping of the CD-ROM disks.

Until recently, few students could go through school without having a lesson in the use of *Readers' Guide to Periodical Literature*. Now instruction in use of periodical indexes has expanded to include *Magazine Index* and CD-ROM indexes such as TOM and NewsBank. The availability of index and full-text information in these formats has greatly expanded a user's ability to find information in newspapers and magazines.

TYPES OF REFERENCE BOOKS

For those with no previous experience in responding to reference questions, descriptions of some basic types of reference books follow. They serve as a quick introduction to the kinds of sources that you will want in your library. The list is not intended as a core reference collection or a basic buying list, although the titles listed were in print at the time this manuscript was written. Rather, these have been chosen because they illustrate one type of reference book from the many types found in libraries.

The first reference books described are basics that would be a first entry point to respond to simple questions, such as dictionaries, atlases, and encyclopedias. Discussion of more specialized reference books follows.

This list may assist you in identifying some of the types of references that you would include in your library. To make your actual selections, you may use selection guides such as those listed in the annotated bibliography; children are exposed to basic beginning reference books as soon as they are able to manipulate the alphabet. Beginning dictionaries and simple encyclopedias have color illustrations, and most of their unabridged counterparts, although they may have some color illustrations such as flags of the countries, have only black-and-white line drawings or photographs. Beginning or abridged dictionaries and encyclopedias also differ in the amount of information given. First dictionaries define only a limited number of words with easy-to-read definitions, and more advanced dictionaries include more words and may include special sections such as foreign language to English or English to a foreign language, basic grammar, and hints for authors, among others.

Dictionaries and Other Guides to Words

Dictionaries are helpful in locating pronunciations and definitions. They range from the unabridged to the very specific to the beginning dictionaries. Even a colorful thesaurus is available for elementary children. Such a variety exists that a large number are cited here just to indicate their diversity. Dictionaries vary in size from small volumes that fit easily into a briefcase or coat pocket to large tomes that are difficult to carry from one desk to another.

A recent publication should assist in the choice of dictionaries for use in schools and children's sections in public libraries:

Kister, Kenneth F. *Kister's Best Dictionaries for Adults & Young People: A Comparative Guide.* Phoenix, Ariz: Oryx Press, 1992. 464pp. $39.50 (ISBN 0-89774-191-9).

This work reviews 300 English language dictionaries from unabridged to pocket dictionaries. A total of 132 are for adults and 168 for children and young students. Entries include title, edition, editors, publisher, date, distributors, number of pages, and price. These entries may be as long as six pages or as short as four lines. Appendixes include Dictionary and Language Associations; Additional Sources for Evaluating Dictionaries; Information Books, Articles, Journals, and Nonprint Materials about Dictionaries; Selected Publications on Language; and Directory of Dictionary Publishers and Distributors. Finally, there are author, title, and subject indexes.

Examples of two beginning dictionaries for the new reader include the following:

The American Heritage Picture Dictionary. Boston: Houghton Mifflin, 1994. 144pp. $10.95 (ISBN 0-395-42531-X).

"Designed to provide the help and encouragement young people need now, in the preschool and early primary years," this dictionary has 600 entries with full-color illustrations that carefully avoid stereotypes.

Eastman, Philip D. *The Cat in the Hat Beginner Book Dictionary.* New York: Random House, 1984. 144pp. $8.95 (LC 64-001157) (ISBN 0-394-810090).

This work contains basic words with simple sentences and humorous illustrations. It is also available in French and Spanish.

For upper elementary or beginning middle school students, one might choose the following:

The Macmillan Dictionary for Children. New York: Macmillan, 1989. 896pp. $14.95 (LC 89-060916) (ISBN 0-027-615618).

This was designed as a beginning dictionary and works well with grades three-five. Its 30,000 entries include some geographic locations.

Unabridged dictionaries are more likely to have an unusual word because they have so many more words defined. However, they do pose the problem often suggested as a joke, "How can I find the word if I can't spell it?" Unabridged dictionaries include the following:

Webster's Third New International Dictionary of the English Language Unabridged. Springfield, Mass.: Merriam-Webster, 1986. 2662pp. $99.95 (ISBN 0-877792-011).

About 450,000 entries are listed in one alphabet. The section "Explanatory Notes" helps you understand the format of entries; for example, definitions are arranged chronologically within each entry. Perhaps one example of a difference between an abridged and an unabridged dictionary would be the 20-page "Guide to Pronunciation." A few black-and-white illustrations, including sketches, symbols, and formulas, are scattered through the three-column pages. For example, page 1090 shows a railway car, "hopper car," and "one form of hopscotch figure."

Weiner, Edmund S., and Joyce M. Hawkins, eds. *Oxford Guide to the English Language.* New York: Oxford University Press, 1986. 608pp. $25.00 (ISBN 0-19-869131-9).

This includes word formation, pronunciation, vocabulary, and grammar but stresses British English.

Some dictionaries cover vocabulary for specialized topics such as those listed below. These reference books define words describing animals, birds, mysticism and the occult, geographical names, science, and politics.

Chinery, Michael, ed. *Dictionary of Animals.* New York: Arco, 1984. 380pp. $17.95 (LC 84-716) (ISBN 0-668-06155-3).

This is designed for the elementary through junior high student, with brief descriptions of animals. Photographs and drawings illustrate many definitions.

Choate, Ernest A. *The Dictionary of American Bird Names.* Rev. ed. Boston: Gambit, 1985. 240pp. $9.95 (ISBN 0-87645-121-0).

Contains both scientific and common names.

Concise Science Dictionary. 2d. ed. New York: Oxford University Press, 1991. (Oxford Paperback Library Series). 768pp. $10.95 paper (ISBN 0-19-286102-6).

Contains 7,000 entries from astronomy, biology, chemistry, computing science, earth sciences, mathematics, and physics.

Freedman, Alan. *The Computer Glossary: The Complete Illustrated Desk Reference.* 7th ed. New York: AMACOM, 1994. 688pp. $39.95 (ISBN 0-814450-047).

This is a business-oriented glossary with 5,300 entries. It is also available in paper-and-disk so that it can be loaded on the library computer for electronic access.

Greenberg, Milton, and Jack C. Plano. *The American Political Dictionary.* 8th ed. Troy, Mo.: Holt, Rinehart & Winston, 1993. 704pp. $20.00 paper (ISBN 0-15-500281-3).

Defines over 1,200 terms and comments on their place in American history and politics; arranged alphabetically by topics. Topics include the U.S. Constitution, civil rights, legislative and judicial processes, business and labor, health, education, foreign policy, and state and local government.

Webster's New Geographical Dictionary. Rev. ed. Springfield, Mass.: Merriam-Webster, 1988. 1568pp. $24.95 (ISBN 0-87779-446-4).

A concise, easy-to-read guide to 47,000 geographical names both ancient and modern, it includes pronunciation, word division, brief descriptions, population statistics, and brief histories. Many charts, lists, and maps are of further assistance.

Other dictionaries may be helpful in answering questions about the language, unusual slang terms, and abbreviations.

Green, Jonathan. *The Dictionary of Contemporary Slang.* Chelsea, Mich.: Scarbrough House, 1985. 334pp. $17.95 (LC 85-40247) (ISBN 0-8128-3051-2).

Includes 11,500 definitions in current use. Slang listings include both definitions and citations to where the word was found.

Morris, William, and Mary Morris. *Harper Dictionary of Contemporary Usage.* New York: Harper & Row, 1992. 672pp. $13.00 paper (LC 83-48797) (ISBN 0-06-272021-X).

A guide to usage and usage problems in English. Both terms and phrases are listed alphabetically. This book is considered one of the most comprehensive dictionaries of American usage available.

Partridge, Eric. *A Dictionary of Slang and Unconventional English: Colloquialisms and Catch-phrases, Solecisms and Catachreses, Nicknames and Vulgarisms.* 8th ed. New York: Macmillan, 1985. 1408pp. $75.00 (ISBN 0-02-594980-2).

This differs from *The Dictionary of Contemporary Slang* in that it deals with the history of words, often no longer used words rather than words in current use.

Webster's Guide to Abbreviations. Springfield, Mass.: Merriam-Webster, 1985. 383pp. $5.95 (ISBN 0-87779-072-8).

As the title states, this is a guide to abbreviations found in ordinary reading, study, or work.

Once you have become familiar with dictionaries, you can turn your attention to encyclopedias.

Encyclopedias

Encyclopedias are suggested as excellent references between the search in the card or online catalog and more in-depth references that take longer to locate. The value of an encyclopedia is that it covers many different topics, albeit with short articles. Encyclopedias have bibliographies that may help with a first search into a topic.

A student to whom you offer an encyclopedia may return it, explaining, "Teacher says we can't use the encyclopedia." Because an encyclopedia does have much helpful information, you may wish to discuss this with the teacher, pointing out that students are cautioned not to copy articles word for word and that the encyclopedia is an excellent first source of information about any topic. Further, the citations listed at the ends of articles are extremely helpful in directing users to more in-depth sources.

Encyclopedias vary by the audience for which they have been developed, length of articles, difficulty of articles in both reading level and concepts, and number of volumes, with the ultimate difference in the purchase cost. They also vary by the method used to update volumes, the accuracy of information provided, and the choice and number of articles revised each year. Reviews of encyclopedias in the professional literature generally compare the new edition to its predecessor as well as to one or more of its competitors.

Encyclopedias should be replaced as often as possible, with new sets purchased *at least every five years*. If the library budget is sufficient, sets from different publishers as well as different years of one encyclopedia may be available. When funds are limited, a more careful choice must be made. Encyclopedias from which to choose include the following. Publication dates are given, but they change regularly, and you must order the most recent edition. They are listed in alphabetical order and not in any rank order for priority purchase.

Collier's Encyclopedia. New York: Collier, 1995. 24 vols., $35 ea. vol. (ISBN 1571610030).

This is excellent for secondary and junior college students, with scholarly, continuously revised articles written to attract a more popular audience than its two competitors. New librarians should understand that they must use the index to locate the specific treatment, as the encyclopedia is arranged under general topics.

Merit Students Encyclopedia. New York: Macmillan Educational Company, 1991. 20 vols., $579 set (ISBN 0029437520).

This one is developed for elementary through high school, although some reviewers consider most of the articles suitable only for junior high and older. Continuously being revised, longer articles match curriculum subjects, and some articles are very short, such as those describing a novel or an organization. This encyclopedia is especially useful in a library with few other reference sources.

New Encyclopaedia Britannica. 15th ed. Chicago: Encyclopaedia Britannica, 1994. 32 vols.

Encyclopeadia Britannica was designed for adult use, featuring a 2-volume index, the *Propaedia*; a 12-volume *Micropedia* described as the "Ready Reference and Index"; and the 17-volume *Macropaedia* or "Knowledge in Depth." The 1985 revision of the original done in 1974 has major changes in numbers of volumes in the *Micropedia* and the *Macropaedia* and in the lengths of articles. This encyclopedia is updated yearly by Britannica World Data and Britannica Book of the Year.

Oxford Illustrated Encyclopedia. Oxford, England: Oxford University Press, 1993. 9 vols. $265.00 set (ISBN 0198692234).

Oxford University Press uses a theme approach, and each volume is independent of the other volumes. The final volume contains the index. Color and black-and-white illustrations add to the general attractiveness of the information.

World Book Encyclopedia. World Book. Annual.

The best-selling encyclopedia today, this is an excellent general encyclopedia for elementary through high school. Although there are some longer articles, many of which fit topics taught in school, most are shorter and the vocabulary is much simpler to read.

Atlases

Atlases are guides to countries and the world. They must be up-to-date or the user will not be able to locate the city, state, or nation of interest. A number of different atlases are available; they vary in several respects, the first being size, which affects storage. Other considerations concern differences in contents.

- Size

Some require an atlas stand or other large surface to open the book, and handling these may be difficult for patrons. Some need to be opened fully to use them, for many maps cover two pages rather than one map to each page.

- Coverage

Some atlases provide historical maps, others cover a single country, some include the world, and others the atmosphere surrounding the Earth. If funds are limited, the volume that includes more countries will serve more users.

- Currency

Perhaps because atlases are so large and so expensive, you may be reluctant to discard them when they should be replaced. However, information in your atlases is supposed to represent the present globe. Copyright dates do not always insure this, so you must look at the African continent or countries such as the former Soviet Union to confirm currency, and then discard those with misinformation. You would not wish to drive cross-country in the United States with an outdated road map, and you certainly would not want a patron to be unable to locate St. Petersburg in the former Soviet Union because your atlas was 10 years old.

- Legibility

Names and symbols on maps must be legible if they are to be easily read.

- Indexes

Recently, geography has become less important in our schools' curricula, and many of today's students have little idea of what continent any country is on, much less any cities, states, counties, or other divisions. For this reason, an excellent index or series of indexes is imperative. The atlases cited below are examples of general atlases of current names and places. You will need to consult library literature for reviews of current atlases before choosing one for purchase. Also, be sure to reanalyze any atlases you have to make certain their information is accurate. You might even note on an atlas page when names of countries or political boundaries are being revised, to alert users.

Bacheller, Martin A., ed. *Ambassador World Atlas*. Maplewood, N.J.: Hammond, 1992. 524pp. $54.95 (ISBN 0-8437-1292-9).
    Includes 112,000 names located by plate number and a grid on each plate. Some 400 full-color maps and charts, gazetteer, locator, economic and physical maps, flags, zip code index, and geographical terms. Almost half of the volume covers the United States. Population data are given for some countries.

Not all atlases are designed to provide current information. The following are examples of atlases that show the world during previous eras.

Adams, James T., ed. *Atlas of American History*. 2d rev. ed. New York: updated. Scribner's, 1985. 306pp. $65.00 (ISBN 0-684-18411-7).
    Includes census data, national developments arranged in chronological order from the exploration of America through colonization to the present. The index includes 5,000 names that are keyed to maps.

Barraclough, Geoffrey. *The Times Concise Atlas of World History*. 3d. ed. 192pp. Maplewood, N.J.: Hammond, 1989. 358pp. $27.95 paper (ISBN 72300-3041-0).
    Includes color maps and charts, a bibliography, and index arranged chronologically from prehistoric times to the present.

Cleveland, William A., ed. *Britannica Atlas*. Chicago: Encyclopaedia Britannica, 1994. 1v. various paging. $109.00 (ISBN 0-85229-606-1).
    Divided into four parts: maps of the world as a whole with thematic maps; graphic representations of world's major oceans, and continents with political boundaries; worldwide data on countries; and indexes to 170,000 names. Well-established, excellent basic reference. Owners of a recent edition of Rand McNally's *New International Atlas* do not need the *Britannica Atlas*; they are virtually identical.

Cussans, Thomas, et al., eds. *The Times Atlas of European History*. New York: Times Books/HarperCollins, 1994. 206pp. $40.00 (ISBN 0-06-270101-0).
    Historical atlas covering European history from 900 B.C. to 1993. Color maps, index of place-names. Maps depict boundaries of states, peoples, religions, other subjects, political divisions, geographical features, and cities and towns.

Ferrell, Robert H., and Richard Natkiel. *Atlas of American History*. Updated ed. New York: Facts on File, 1993. 192pp. $29.95 (ISBN 0-8160-2883-4).
    Includes census data, national developments arranged in chronological order from the exploration of America through colonization to the present. Includes 250 original maps and diagrams.

Shepherd, William R. *Shepherd's Historical Atlas*. 9th ed., rev. New York: Barnes & Noble, 1980. 348pp. $35.95 (LC 64-26) (ISBN 0-389-201155-3, N6671).
    Ancient times from Greece, the Mycenian Period, and the Orient (1450 B.C.) to modern United States and Europe.

Once you have learned how to look up items in dictionaries, encyclopedias, and atlases, you will begin to learn other reference books to help you find answers quickly. Almanacs are excellent sources of brief answers to questions.

Almanacs

The following are the two most often used almanacs: *Information Please Almanac and Yearbook*. New York: McGraw-Hill, 1947- (annual). $21.95; $8.95 paper. *World Almanac and Book of Facts*. New York: Press Pub Co. (The New York World): 1923- (annual). $19.95; $8.95 paper. As indicated, both are published annually. Their tables of contents reveal that they have similar but different information. Although both have information concerning elections, *World Almanac* has "Top 10 News Stories," and *Information Please Almanac* covers "The Year in Pictures." *Information Please Almanac* also has color maps and illustrations, a crossword puzzle guide, the most important scientific theories and discoveries from the fifteenth century to the present, and an article on "How to make wise investment decisions." *World Almanac* features major actions of the U.S. Congress; major decisions of the U.S. Supreme Court—1989-1990; names, addresses, and telephone numbers of congressional representatives; and flags and maps of countries.

Both are being challenged by a newcomer, *The Universal Almanac*, John W. Wright, ed. Kansas City, Mo.: Andrews and McMeel, 1993. 720pp. $12.95 paper (ISBN 0-83-628032-6). A review in *Wilson Library Bulletin*, January, 1991 (27), states:

> Readable, visually appealing, and competitively priced, it lacks the variety of information found in *World Almanac*, but its greater depth makes it worth purchasing. For example . . . it was the only source among the four [tested] to include short descriptions of the work of all Nobel Prize winners in all categories; the rest just provided the winners' names.

Whatever your choices, to have instant information that is up-to-date, your almanacs should be purchased annually. Many school librarians retain back issues to use in teaching students how to use the almanac. However, be sure to remind users that information from previous volumes may be dated.

The reference cited below is an example of a specialized almanac, designed for use by secretaries but containing information of use to you if you are called by someone whose secretary does not have *The Secretary's Almanac and Fact Book*.

DeVries, Mary A. *Complete Secretary's Handbook*. 6th ed. Englewood Cliffs, N.J.: Prentice-Hall, 1993. 576pp. $39.95 (ISBN 0-13-59666-7).

It contains basic tenets of secretarial practice; facts and reference material necessary to modern businesses including postal, telegraph, and telephone service; a global time chart; international dialing codes; major U.S. airports, passport agencies, national agencies and offices; copyright guidelines; manuscript editing; library classification systems; a foreign money table; and IRS tax publications and forms. An alphabetical index is included in the back, and the table of contents includes a chronological listing of entries.

Handbooks

Information seekers in specialized areas may appreciate a reference that contains a wide variety of data in their field. Handbooks are good ready reference tools to meet that need. The examples given below are from the field of math and science.

Beyer, William H., ed. *Handbook of Mathematical Sciences*. 6th ed. West Palm Beach, Fla.: CRC Press, 1987. 992pp. $84.95 (ISBN 0-8493-0656-6).

Eberhart, George M., comp. *The Whole Library Handbook: Current Data, Professional Advice, and Curiosa About Libraries and Library Services*. Chicago: American Library Association, 1995. 521pp. $30.00 paper (LC 94-42091) (ISBN 0-8389-0646-X).
This includes much you need to know about libraries, the profession, materials, operations, special populations, public relations, technology, issues (including intellectual freedom and access, legislation, literacy, copyright, ethics, and international concerns), and librariana (trivia; anecdotes; facetiae; satire; rubber stamps; postcards; unusual authors, titles, subject headings; librarians on film; worst serial title changes; and stamps).

Lide, David R., and Christina Martin, eds. *Handbook of Chemistry & Physics*. 74th ed. Boca Raton, Fla.: CRC Press, 1993. various pricing. (ISBN 0-8493-0474-1).
This handbook, revised annually, contains tables for mathematics, elements, compounds (inorganic and organic), general chemistry, formulas, data for planets, among others.

Yearbooks

Hunter, Brian, ed. *The Statesman's Yearbook, 1994-95*, 131st ed. New York: St. Martin's Press, 1993. 1730pp. $89.95 (ISBN 0-312-09701-8).
A standard reference for all types of libraries, it contains updated information on international organizations and countries of the world. For larger countries, statistics are provided on states, provinces, and territories within the country, as well as information on religion, education, history, social welfare, politics, and economics. A brief history is given for each country.

Statistical Abstract of the United States, 1993. 113th ed. Austin, Tex.: Reference Press, 1993. 980pp. $19.95 paper (ISBN 1878753312).
This volume contains a wide variety of numerical facts about the United States, such as imports, exports, population.

Directories

Directories provide location information for persons seeking help in a particular area for a particular problem. It may mean locating nursing homes, association addresses, or manufacturing companies, among others. Directories often include a wide variety of information about their subject, such as calendars of activities and addresses of peripheral agencies, groups, or organizations. The examples below show a variety of directories leading you to information about higher education.

Anderson, Marcia J., and Barbara A. Schmidt. *Directory of Degree Programs in Nursing: Baccalaureate, Master's, Doctoral.* New York: Arco, 1984. 320pp. $29.95 (ISBN 0-668-05757-2).
 This includes 501 nursing schools selected and sent surveys. For nonrespondents, only the name and address are given. For the others, information includes name of the chairperson, telephone number, degrees offered, accreditation, admission requirements, contact person, and a brief description of the program.

The College Handbook. New York: College Entrance Examination Board, 1993. 2000pp. $20.00 paper (ISBN 0-87447-479-5).
 Provides information on selecting a college, how to apply, and financial aid considerations; also lists, alphabetically by state, 3,000 two-year and four-year institutions. A second alphabet gives college name. The index includes state location as well as page numbers.

Dilts, Susan, and Mark Zidzik, eds. *Peterson's Guide to Four-Year Colleges, 1994.* 24th ed. Princeton, N.J.: Peterson's Guides, 1993. 2740 pp. $18.95 paper (ISBN 1-56079-235-3).
 Most useful to students in grades 10, 11, and 12 and their parents. This guide to undergraduate education in both two- and four-year institutions is also available in several online databases and in CD-ROM. Selection of institution, financial aid, standardized tests, and college majors are discussed. Colleges are listed geographically, by difficulty of entrance requirements, by ranges, and by majors. For each college, information includes size, costs, housing, programs, and campus life, a two-page description of the college, and a full description of Air Force and Army ROTC programs.

O'Neill, Joseph P. *Corporate Tuition Aid Programs: A Directory of College Financial Aid for Employees at America's Largest Corporations.* 2d ed. Princeton, N.J.: Peterson's Guides, 1986. 214pp. $7.50 paper (LC 86-62353) (ISBN 0-87866-482-3).
 Based on a survey of Fortune 1000 companies, with 655 responding. Companies are listed alphabetically, and information includes eligibility requirements, amount of aid provided, and any limitations.

Yale Daily News Staff. *Insider's Guide to the Colleges, 1993.* New York: St. Martin's Press, 1993. 768pp. $26.95 (ISBN 0-312-08507-9); $15.99 paper (ISBN 0-312-08244-X).
 Written and edited by students who "tell what their colleges are really like." Based on reviews of 270 colleges and universities, information is given alphabetically by state, then by institution and includes enrollment, percentage of applicants accepted, tuition, size of library, median ACT and SAT scores, and fraternity and sorority participation.

Lest you be led to believe that all directories are related to college entrance or financial aid to students who wish to become further educated after high school, the following is cited:

Brownson, Ann L., ed. *Congressional Staff Directory, 1994-2: With Biographical Information on Members & Key Congressional Staff*, 42d ed. Mount Vernon, Va.: Staff Directories, 1994. 1312pp. $69.00 paper (ISBN 087289102X).
Contains not only names, addresses, and telephone numbers of U.S. Congress members and their staffs but also biographical information on staffs. It also includes the staff at the congressional party organizations, the Library of Congress, and the General Accounting Office.

Biographies

Information about famous and infamous persons is found in single volumes devoted to the hero or heroine. Collections exist of brief biographies about related individuals, such as presidents of the United States, women in history, and sports figures, among others. These usually provide more information than can be found in encyclopedias, but entire biographies, collected biographies, or encyclopedia articles are not available on everyone about whom your patrons are seeking information. Examples of reference books with brief information about many persons include the following:

Current Biography Yearbook, 19 —. New York: H. W. Wilson, 19 —. Annual. $52.00 (ISSN 0011-3344).
Issued in periodical format each month and accumulated in hard cover annually. Persons are listed alphabetically; one or more columns with pictures are devoted to each person. Each volume is indexed by profession.

Downs, Robert B., John T. Flanagan, and Harold W. Scott. *More Memorable Americans 1750-1950*. Littleton, Colo.: Libraries Unlimited, 1985. 397pp. $30.00 (LC 84-27780) (ISBN 0-87287-421-4).
This work lists 151 persons in politics, arts, entertainment, business, science, education, and the military. Entries are brief but contain major achievements and references to further information.

Gareffa, Peter M., ed. *Contemporary Newsmakers, 1987: A Biographical Guide to People in the News*. Detroit: Gale Research, 1988. 440pp. $85.00 (ISBN 0-8103-2203); *The New York Times Biographical Service: A Compilation of Current Biographical Information of General Interest*. New York: *New York Times*; and *Current Biography* (previously reported) are all three serials with monthly or quarterly publications.

International Who's Who. 54th ed. Washington, D.C.: Taylor & Francis, 1990. 1700pp. $250.00 (ISBN 0-946653-58-5).
A list of 15,000 persons in high public office all over the world, including royal families.

Simpson, Kieran, ed. *Canadian Who's Who, 1992.* Toronto: University of Toronto Press, 1992. 1219pp. $160.00 (ISBN 0-8020-4670-3).

A guide to 8,000 Canadians who are politicians; persons in business, sports, art, media, and academia; as well as religious leaders.

Webster's New Biographical Dictionary. Springfield, Mass.: Merriam-Webster, 1988. 1147pp. $24.95 (ISBN 0-87779-543-6).

This contains brief biographies of 40,000 persons from all periods of history and all nations. Emphasis is given to heads of state and American and British persons.

Who's Who Among American High School Students. Annual. Lake Forest, Ill.: Educational Communications.

Produced for nine regions of the United States, the volumes include juniors and seniors attending 22,000 national public, private, and parochial high schools who are nominated for academic excellence and leadership in curricular and extracurricular activities. Some information is given on preparing for the SAT, seeking financial aid for college, and choosing a college major. School librarians will wish to purchase a copy when students from their school are regularly listed.

Who's Who in America. Wilmette, Ill.: Marquis Who's Who.

This lists 75,000 persons in the United States, Canada, and Mexico who hold federal, state, and local offices; are military officers; officials in major universities; officers in businesses; heads of cultural, educational, religious, and scientific organizations; or have received major awards. Data include name, occupation, vital statistics, names of parents, marriage, children, education, professional certifications, career, writings, civic and political activities, awards, professional memberships, political affiliation, religion, clubs, and home and business addresses. Regional volumes similar to this include *Who's Who in the East, Who's Who in the Midwest,* and *Who's Who in the South and Southwest.*

Who's Who in America: Student Version, 1989-91. Wilmette, Ill.: Marquis Who's Who, 1989. 4 vols., $79.00 (ISBN 0-8379-1250-4).

Genealogy, or biographical information about our ancestors, is becoming ever more interesting in the United States. One could speculate that this is of interest to older, retired persons who have the time, interest, and money to travel to their roots as well as the desire to do the research. Another reason might be the lack of permanency of much of our population. Perhaps there is a sense of need to solidify a place in the universe. It may be that sources are more readily available, or that librarians are better at sending researchers to the appropriate sources. Whatever the reason, you may be asked to suggest sources of local information about families who lived in your area in the past. If you are not the repository of such documentation, you should locate the agencies that are. A handy list of the types of records available in each agency, the names and addresses of the persons to contact, and the hours the facilities are open will be helpful. You may need to confirm the assistance these agencies can provide, for many have very small staffs and little money to mail responses to requests for information.

Bibliographies and Indexes

Bibliographies and indexes list items on special topics. They are obviously most useful when you have copies of those items that they reference. Bibliographies also are more useful when there is easy access to the materials cited. You need to identity those items cited in your bibliographies that you own. Users will become frustrated if they are given a source with what seems to be a vast array of choices when, in reality, their choices are limited because few of the books cited are immediately available in your library. You may wish to pencil in call numbers, so that patrons need not look in your card catalog or online public access catalog to see if items are in your library or to locate call numbers for titles that are on your shelves. This means that you must keep this information up-to-date, for both additions to your collection and deletions when an indexed item is lost or must be removed from the shelf for any other reason. This process is greatly simplified when you have an online public access catalog.

If you have an extensive collection of bibliographies and a small collection of materials, you will become a heavy borrower from other libraries through interlibrary loan. To go beyond your holdings, you will access any records you have of the members of your consortium through any bibliographic databases, or you may search in something as broad as the Library of Congress National Union Catalog, although few small libraries need this reference. Made up of many volumes, it not only is expensive to purchase, but also occupies several shelves of any library. Some examples of less extensive bibliographies include the following:

Enser, A. G. *A Subject Bibliography of the Second World War: Books in English 1975-1987*. Brookfiels, Vt.: Gower, 1990. 287pp. $59.95 (ISBN 0-566-05736-0).

This work contains only book citations rather than periodical literature, poetry, fiction, or juvenile works, and all have been published from 1975-1983. The author has also published *A Subject Bibliography of the First World War: Books in English 1914; A Subject Bibliography of the Second World War and Aftermath: Books in English 1975-1987*, and *A Subject Bibliography of the First World War: Books in English, 1914-1978*.

Indexes provide access to books in your library and help you find the contents without having to type extensive sets of cards for the card catalog or make reference entries for your online public access catalog. Examples of indexes are *Index to Children's Poetry* and *Granger's Index to Poetry*. These authors gathered books of collected poetry by many authors, called anthologies, or poetry books by a single author and noted the authors' names, the titles of the poems, and a subject index. Users can locate a poem by a favorite poet, a poem by its title, or any poem about a specific topic such as one of the seasons, children, friendship, or a particular animal, among others. These also include an index to the first line of any poem, in case that is what a patron trying to locate a particular poem remembers.

Brewton, John E., and Sara W. Brewton. *Index to Children's Poetry*. New York: H. W. Wilson.

This book is irregularly published, but is available in a main volume with supplements. The anthologies indexed between with poetry published in 1935. The Brewtons have also included an indication of the grade level.

Granger, Edith. *Granger's Index to Poetry*. New York: Columbia University Press, irregularly published in several editions beginning with anthologies published since 1904.

Again, note that an index is more valuable if the books indexed are in your library. When you own an indexed title, place the call number for the volume in the front with the listing of books indexed.

To this point, this chapter has discussed reference use of published bibliographies. Creating your own bibliographies of your library's holdings will be discussed in chapter 6 under services.

SPECIALIZED INFORMATION

References cited here include books that would be appropriate in either reference or regular collection. Patrons may enjoy a leisurely look at them as well as using them to answer ready reference questions. A book such as *Anniversaries and Holidays* (see below) is very popular with those doing newsletters or putting up bulletin boards regularly, because it gives information on seasonal and traditional happenings. Certainly the *Guinness Book of World Records* is entertaining for all ages.

Adams, James T. *Album of American History*. Rev. ed. New York: Scribner's, 1981. 3 vols. $290.00 (LC 74-91746) (ISBN 0-684-16848-0).

This is available in two editions, the first published in 1981 and a six-volume updated version in 1985. Each volume includes an era of history and provides black-and-white illustrations of the American scene, including Vietnam, social consciousness, U.S. business, ecological awareness, architecture, and daily life.

Cook, Chris. *Facts on File World Political Almanac*. New York: Facts on File, 1995. 643pp. $40.00 (ISBN 0-8160-2338-9).

Gregory, Ruth W. *Anniversaries and Holidays*. Chicago: American Library Association, 1983. 260pp. $30.00 (LC 83-3784) (ISBN 0-8389-0389-4).

This work lists, in calendar form, 1,690 religious and other holidays as well as special event days for 152 countries. Birthdays of 1,046 important people add to the usefulness of this volume in identifying special days for celebration. Annotated bibliographies cover information about some of the holidays.

Gunston, Bill. *An Illustrated Guide to the Modern U.S. Air Force*. New York: Prentice-Hall, 1984. 160pp. $10.95 paper (ISBN 0-668-05497-2).

This is one of several illustrated military guides, including the Navy, the former Soviet Union's Air Force, Navy, and Ground Forces, and Israel's Air Force. It is well illustrated with color illustrations and includes descriptions of weapons systems— size of crew, armor, dimensions, weight, performance, and history and development.

Harris, Bill, ed. *The Congressional Medal of Honor*. Avenal, N.J.: Outlet Book, 1990. $15.99 (ISBN 0-517693-23-2).

This contains citations for the award of the Medal of Honor, grouped into 22 sections by war, campaign, conflict, or era.

Kane, Joseph Nathan. *Famous First Facts: A Record of First Happenings, Discoveries, and Inventions in American History*. 4th ed. New York: H. W. Wilson, 1981. 1350pp. $80.00 (ISBN 0-8242-0661-4).

This volume contains 9,000 firsts in American life.

Krause, Chester L., and Clifford Mishler. *Standard Catalog of World Coins, 1991*. 17th ed. Iola, Wis.: Krause Publications, 1990. 1920pp. $36.95 paper (LC 79-640940) (ISBN 0-87341-136-6).

This is an annual with general information about coins from ancient times to the present. Includes detailed information about recent coins from all countries and from 1793 for U.S. coins.

Literary Market Place, 1995. New York: R. R. Bowker, 1994—. Annual. (ISBN 0-8352-3475-4).

This lists 20,000 persons and companies involved in publishing in the United States and Canada. It is arranged under "book publishing," "book clubs, rights, and representatives," "associations and other organizations," "book trade events, conferences, and courses" "literary awards, contests, and grants," "services and suppliers," "direct mail promotion," "book review, selection, and reference," "radio and television," "wholesale, export, and import," "book manufacturing," and "magazine and newspaper publishing." Further information includes each publishing company's shipping address, ISBN prefix, year founded, publishing profile, foreign representatives, regional sales offices, advertising agency, number of titles in print, and number of titles published in the present year. Related information includes the publisher's imprint, affiliated companies, subsidiaries, divisions, and any special distribution arrangements. This book will help you respond to patrons who wish to sell their creative writing. Many fledgling authors see a librarian as someone who can judge their work for its possibilities for publishing. You will be wise to give them a handbook on how to write for publication or offer them a reference book such as this to guide them to the appropriate publisher.

McFarlan, Donald. *Guinness Book of World Records*. Annual.

This is one of the most popular reference books available. The world's records are given for a wide variety of events. In the new volume, all eating records are being removed to halt participation in rather dangerous contests.

Magill, Frank N., ed. *Masterplots*. Englewood Cliffs, N.J.: Salem Press. Various dates.

This is a reference that has grown in size over the years. Originally it was in one volume; you may now choose from the following partial listing:

1976, 12 vols., 7358pp. $425.00 (ISBN 0-89356-025-1);

1985, rev. ed., (American Fiction Series) 3 vols., 1485pp. $120.00 (ISBN 0-89356-500-8);

1985, rev. ed., (British Fiction Series) 3 vols., 1790pp. $120.00 (ISBN 0-89356-504-0).

Masterplots II, 1990, (Drama Series) 4 vols., 1804pp. $325.00 (ISBN 0-89356-491-5).

Some librarians think that they should lock up references such as Cliffs Notes and *Masterplots,* so that students cannot use them in place of actually reading the assigned novel, short story, or play. However, a teacher who makes an assignment that can be completed using this type of abbreviated reference should not have made the assignment in the first place.

Mossman, Jennifer, ed. *Holidays and Anniversaries of the World: A Compre- hensive Catalogue Containing Detailed Information on Every Month and Day of the Year.* 2d ed. Detroit: Gale Research, 1989. 1080pp. $85.00 (ISBN 0-8103-4870-5).

This contains 23,000 regional, national, and international holidays and anniversaries for each of the 366 days and each month of the Gregorian year. At the beginning of each month, the history, origin of the name, and special holidays, commemorations, and events are given. Included for each day are birth dates of famous persons, historical events, saints' days, and other holy days. Major holidays and observances are also given. Its cost makes it less likely to be found in the small collection, but it is of great value to the elementary or secondary school librarian needing to produce bulletin boards or suggested activity lists for teachers.

Scott Standard Postage Stamp Catalogue. New York: Scott Publishing, 19—. Annual. 4 vols., $49.95 ea.

This reference lists international stamps by various governments, giving both date of issue and value. Although this and *Standard Catalog of World Coins* are reference books, they will be perused over and over by collectors or would-be collectors.

Talbert, Richard J. *Atlas of Classical History.* New York: Routledge, Chapman & Hall, 1989. 224pp. $18.50 (ISBN 0-415-03463-9).

Written for high school and college students, this book is in chronological order from the Bronze Age to the time of Constantine. Maps are accompanied by double-columned texts including town plans, archaeological sites, language areas of Greece and Rome, trade routes, religious centers, wars, military cam- paigns and battles, exploration and colonization, extent of alliances, kingdoms, empires, and frontiers.

Quotation Books

Quotation books are most often used by persons who are preparing a presentation and wish to find a good quotation.

Byrne, Robert. *The Third—And Possibly Best—637 Best Things Anybody Ever Said.* New York: Fawcett Book Group, 1986. 190pp. $4.95 paper (ISBN 0-449- 20762-5).

Arranged by broad subject areas. Although this is a fun book to read, it is well documented and could be used by the patron wishing to add a clever quote to a speech or paper.

Farber, Bernard E. *A Teacher's Treasury of Quotations.* Jefferson, N.C.:
 McFarland, 1985. 384pp. $39.95 (LC 84-43218) (ISBN 0-89950-150-8).
 Includes 4,600 education-related quotations with well-documented sources
arranged by 450 specific topics. Topics are listed in a detailed table of contents.

Sampson, Anthony, and Sally Sampson. *The Oxford Book of Ages.* New York:
 Oxford University Press, 1988. 224pp. $7.95 paper (ISBN 0-19-0282244-6).
 Includes quotations written about a certain age or written by the author at
a certain age.

Fund-Raising

The Foundation Directory. New York: Foundation Center. Annual.
 Useful to identify sources of funding from 4,400 foundations, listed by state.

Accuracy of response to questions, as discussed early in this chapter, is
essential. Care must be taken to see that correct information is always provided.
Research has shown that many persons who use libraries are not given full and
accurate information. This problem is sometimes caused when the librarian does
not understand enough about the question to choose a reliable source, uses an
outdated source of information, or does not give a complete explanation. Other
times the librarian looking up the answer does not understand the question.

ONLINE AND CD-ROM REFERENCES

Newspapers and periodicals on CD-ROM have been discussed earlier in
this chapter. Encyclopedias, available with interactive video and sound, also
provide quick access to information. The user can decide whether to read a
speech by John F. Kennedy or see and hear him delivering the speech. Musical
scores are transformed into full orchestral renditions. It is truly a magical
reference source. The articles in encyclopedias can be downloaded to a word-
processing program, allowing the user to add the information to the paper being
written without the laborious and tedious effort of copying and reentering.

Spell-check programs are part of most word-processing programs. *Books
in Print* and *Dissertations Abstracts* are also available on CD-ROM. All of these
serve to replace paper copies of reference sources. The cost of some may be less
on CD-ROM than in paper copy. The only problem is having the equipment to
play back the reference source.

ADDING REFERENCE MATERIALS
TO YOUR COLLECTION

Selecting materials for your collection will be discussed in chapter 7. However, note that reference books are usually expensive, and you do not wish to spend your budget on tools that will not be used. Yet, you are responsible for securing those that will help you and your users answer their information needs. One excellent review source of reference books is the following:

Reference Books Bulletin: A Compilation of Evaluations Appearing in Reference Books Bulletin. Annual. Chicago: American Library Association.

Includes all reviews from *RBB* within the indicated dates arranged under format (bibliographies, dictionaries, encyclopedias, etc.) alphabetically by title. Reviews of online reference tools and works appearing only in microform are included.

DETERMINING WHAT THE USER
REALLY WANTS TO KNOW

To find correct, suitable answers to reference questions, you must take great care to understand the actual question being asked. The patron who asks for information on chickens needs to be queried further to find out if the ultimate goal is raising chickens, checking the legality of cock fighting, getting rid of a neighbor's chickens being cooped illegally, cooking chicken, trying to find out how many chicken farmers are in the area so a new kind of chicken feed can be marketed, seeking a picture of a chicken to create a poster, or determining the effects of salmonella from eating chicken.

Even experienced reference librarians sometimes cannot find enough information to satisfy the patron's request. When a response is not available in the library, another librarian may be called. If much more information is needed than is available in your library, direct the patron to other possible sources of information, either nearby libraries or a designated reference library in the region or state. When the patron can wait, request materials through interlibrary loan. The primary concern is answering most patrons' questions correctly and quickly.

NOTE

1. American Library Association Filing Committee, *ALA Filing Rules*. Chicago: American Library Association, 1980.

GLOSSARY

Definitions are from Young, Heartsill, ed. *The ALA Glossary Terms*. Chicago: American Library Association, 1983.

Abstract. An abbreviated, accurate representation of a work, usually without added interpretation or criticism.

Citation. A note referring to a work from which a passage is quoted or to some source as authority for a statement or proposition.

Full text database. A database in which the data consist of the full text of one or more works.

Main entry. The access point to a bibliographic record by which the bibliographic item is to be uniformly identified and cited.

Chapter 6

SERVICES

Your services reflect the activities offered to serve your patrons with the information they need. Services are designed to enhance the usefulness of the library's information resources for the clientele you are expected to serve. You have analyzed your community and are aware of the characteristics of this target population. You have some ideas about what they want from the library. Their needs dictate how you will help them find and use that information. In addition, you will decide other ways the library can serve them.

Because two universal perceptions are that all libraries and information centers circulate materials and provide reference services, anyone accepting a position in a library is, by tradition if not by necessity, obligated to circulate materials and answer reference questions. Both circulation and reference are described fully in chapters 4 and 5, respectively. Activities beyond those two basic services will be discussed here. You will be deciding to choose from other traditional and perhaps not so traditional information services.

The number, sophistication, and variety of services to be offered depend on size, expertise, and creativity of staff; number of potential users; hours the facility is available to clientele; size of facility; and size and depth of collection, but most of all on stated and perceived needs of patrons. This chapter will discuss existing services that should be continued at the same level, increased, or decreased, and what to do when new services are needed. Help will be given to decide which of your present services you can reduce or stop altogether and which you must continue to offer when different services are needed. You will make decisions in the context of what you can do with existing resources. Finally, methods will be suggested to determine which additional resources will be needed if funding is provided for new or expanded services.

DETERMINING SERVICES TO OFFER

Your users will expect to receive those services they know are offered in your library. You will need to understand what these are in relation to other services that seem to be needed by fewer patrons. It is not only more rewarding to offer services that are perceived as needed by most users, but also services that are not essential, will be ignored by patrons, or, used by very few. To be most effective in providing access to information, you ask your clientele what they perceive as essential and necessary.

DECISION ONE: To analyze present and potential services needed.

This is a multistep process.

- Review services presently offered.

- Evaluate their quality and cost, setting them into priority order.

- Analyze what other services would be useful that are not offered, and prioritize their importance.

- Determine their cost.

- Review present budget to see what old services must be reduced or removed to make room for new services.

This process begins with a review of all the services presently offered to determine if they are helpful and meeting patron needs. If they are not, you will need to analyze which services are not well publicized, well executed, or, perhaps what may be most difficult to acknowledge, no longer helpful.

ACTION ONE: What services are presently offered?

If you have little concept of library services, take the following steps:

- Check the procedures manual to see what basic services are outlined there. An indication of the amount of time devoted to each service may be part of this explanation.

- Ask any clerical staff about users and their use of the library.

- Interview users to get their perceptions of services offered by the library.

Some services are basic, found in almost all libraries, and others may be unique to one type of library or one group of users within a library. Reference service and circulation of materials are examples of basic services, and genealogy research may be available as a specialized service used by a much smaller population of clients.

You asked administrators what they expected during the initial interview and when you began your job. This can be the starting point of your analysis of services. You can begin to confirm their suggestions for old or new services when you review the procedures manual and when you talk with other staff members.

Clerical staff can describe the types of services they have observed or have participated in providing. Volunteers who have worked in the library can also explain how they have helped patrons.

Asking users what they have used and evaluating the success of those services is another way to research the question, "What services should I offer?" Clients themselves may confirm services they have received from the library and what they expect from you. You may wish to provide them with a list of services to help them remember their uses of the library.

ACTION TWO: What services could be offered?

For purposes of discussion, services are described in several configurations. The first are services that provide users direct or indirect access. Direct or immediate access is provided by the following:

- Circulation of all formats, fiction and nonfiction
- Browsing collection
- Ready reference collection
- Developing bibliographies of library holdings
- Providing special collections upon request
- Database searching
- Photocopying

Indirect access includes services from which the client might have delayed rather than immediate access to material, such as

- In-depth reference searches
- Interlibrary loan

Categories of services also can be divided into types of programs. Programs can be

- designed for both passive and active participation by users;
- offered in-house and externally (away from the library);
- collection-related or librarian-oriented services; and
- aimed at specific audiences, e.g., children's, young adult, or adult services.

This programming list is far from all-inclusive in any single division. You should add to the list or delete those not applicable to your library as you begin to analyze what you are presently offering. If you do not offer any service externally, you need not be concerned with interlibrary loan. However, few libraries exist in a vacuum, and it is likely that you will have services in each of the categories.

Programming

Programming can be passive or active. These services differentiate between passive activities of patrons—individually viewing, listening, or reading from the collection with little interaction with the librarian—and active participation in crafts, programs, or book discussions.

Passive participation includes the following:

Reader's guidance, with the librarian making suggestions

Teaching library skills, with the librarian teaching

Films

Storytelling by storytellers

Parenting activities

Summer reading programs

Presentations in the library such as
    book authors

travelogues
awareness presentations such as
    completing an income tax form
    health-related information
    how to do (almost anything)

Active participation includes such activities as the following:

Book discussion groups

Chess tournaments

Crafts demonstrations

In-House and External Services

Services also can be divided between those offered in-house and those designed for clientele outside the library. In-house means the service is provided within the information agency, and external services are provided outside the facility at a service club, day care or senior citizen center, hospital, or other location.

Examples of in-house services:

- Access to collections, including all formats: books, magazines, media, and others

- Reference

- Research packages

- Database searches

- Access to computers, copy machines

- Literacy programs

- Translation

- Special collections: genealogy, local history, among others

- Interlibrary loan

- Local production of audiovisual materials

- Films

- Speakers

Internal or in-house services as listed above include reference. Because reference has been discussed in chapter 5, this service is not repeated here.

Access to collections, including all formats of materials, means you must provide comfortable reading areas, tables, desks, or study carrels on which to work; equipment such as copy machines, microfiche readers, and printers, and projectors that work well; darker areas for viewing films or slides; and facilities for listening to records or tapes quietly. All public areas of your library should be open to all patrons. Care must be taken that "artificial" barriers are not created for circulation items. That is, storage areas behind closed doors inadvertently close items to ready access by users and may appear to hamper open access to information. You may even interpret "access" as providing both the results of a search and the actual materials. For example, upon patron request, you may collect research packages. You research all the materials you have on a topic and all you can collect from other sources within the established time frame. You then send or deliver the items to your patron or tell the patron they are available and where and when to collect them.

Online database searching is most often conducted by staff rather than patron. Because of the costs of connect time, it is well to have an experienced searcher do the actual search. However, because many databases are now available on CD-ROM programs that are user-friendly, you should encourage patrons to conduct their own CD-ROM database searches. In some locations you may need to place time limits on searching if one patron monopolizes the equipment.

Most libraries offer access to computers and copy machines at the present time. The discussion of access to computers for word processing, database management, and spreadsheets is a managerial decision. However, once you have made that decision, you need to decide which software programs are available in-house and to anticipate when patrons will prefer bringing in their own programs to use. Problems arising from computer viruses are considerations with public computers that use disks from other locations.

Literacy programs are often housed in the public library. These new reader programs match trained literacy teachers with illiterate adults. Libraries are nonthreatening environments where adults can visit without having a stigma attached. Most such programs are not your teaching responsibility, nor will you be expected to recruit volunteer tutors or identify illiterates. Your major role will be to provide quiet, private rooms where adult and tutor meet. If literacy programs are to be a service in your public library, you must pay attention to the selection of materials to support the new reader program.

Academic or special libraries are more apt to provide foreign language translation services for clientele who have materials they wish to use in a language they cannot read. In a public library, when the need arises, a translation service rather than in-house translators can be used. You may wish to maintain a list of those in your community who are willing to translate a document upon request, including the fee assessed if it is someone outside your staff.

Local production of audiovisual materials begins with sign-making kits that allow users to prepare anything from a simple microcomputer-generated banner to a garden club fund-raising poster created with sophisticated photographic equipment. Your library may have desktop publishing capabilities that would permit organizations to publish their newsletters. Also, the ability to videotape proceedings such as city council meetings would be helpful to interested users.

Special collections of materials may be available in your library. If the library is in an area where it is the logical repository of local history materials and information on special topics and local individuals, you should plan for housing and access to these materials. You may also be the beneficiary of materials donated by a collector of specialized subject matter. When special collections are housed in a library, the presence of these materials is well publicized and added to state and national databases. Users outside your library jurisdiction can access the materials on location or through interlibrary loan. Providing access to such collections may be a major part of your library service.

Genealogy was discussed in chapter 5 under reference, biographical information. It is repeated here because this topic has become increasingly popular, and governmental agencies with records are besieged by requests from individuals seeking information about their ancestors. These agencies are responsible for recording information, but they usually have small staffs with little time to do in-depth research based on often incorrect or inaccurate dates or spelling of names. When you and your staff cannot do such searches, you should maintain a list of others in the community who can. When your library is the depository of such records, training volunteers to help searchers can relieve your staff of some responsibilities.

Local history collections may be housed in the public or school library, depending on the size of the community. In many small towns, the only library may be in the high school. It is important that archives tracing the history of the area be maintained. If you are assigned this responsibility, you may need to ask the state library for advice on techniques for materials preservation and maintenance of records so that materials can be retrieved.

Interlibrary loan is available for users today through their libraries. The internal aspect includes your request for your patron to another library. You need to understand the forms to complete, the method of communicating requests among agencies, the next library in the communication linkup, and any requirements for the process. If a consortium has been established, steps will be outlined to conduct interlibrary loan requests. For example, if materials are not available in the local library, the consortium is the first step in the chain. If the material is not available in the consortium, a nearby research library may be called to see if the item is there. If not, then the item may be requested from the state library or, finally, from another location.

These procedures have been established to help find the item as close to the requesting library as possible and to dissuade users from expecting that a larger library should always be the first asked to send the material. In fact, it has been shown that a smaller library with the needed material in its collection is more likely to have the item on the shelf than a much larger library with many more patrons.

Films and videotapes are circulated from the library or shown in the library. Noon-hour screenings in libraries near businesses or office complexes have been popular with working patrons who come to watch a program with their bag lunches. They meet and eat while enjoying the showing. Films, videotapes, and filmstrips may also be a part of the storytelling session.

Speakers may be invited to present programs in the library. Early in planning you will need to determine the amount of funding available for an honorarium and travel expenses. Local speakers may be less costly, for they will incur lower transportation costs. Another consideration is where the program will be held. Not all libraries have an auditorium or room big enough for large audiences, and you must consider this when inviting someone to speak. Reservations may be needed so people are not turned away.

Whether your speaker comes for little or no fee or is very costly, you treat the presenter as an honored guest. Your audience will benefit if you are a gracious host. Most speakers need to know the anticipated size of the audience, in case they are preparing materials for distribution or wish to use media to illustrate their talk. You will also want to tell the speaker if someone will be available to help project or distribute materials.

When planning adult programming in a public library, you will also want to consider who your audience is and when they can conveniently attend a program. Many adults come to the library to bring their children, and they may be encouraged to attend an adult event at that time. Otherwise, library programs must compete with patrons' other choices of clubs, tennis, golf, church activities, household chores, and distractions when more than one family member works outside the home.

Examples of external services:

- Circulation

- Telephone reference

- Senior citizen centers

- Lending equipment

- Fax services

- Interlibrary loan, including fax services

- Presentations at meetings of civic organizations

Because circulation services were covered in chapter 4, they will not be discussed here. However, circulation of materials, as the mechanism used to allow items to leave the library, is a major external function.

Telephone reference service makes it possible for users away from the library to call for answers to questions. Most telephone services are used for quick answers to one or two questions. To provide answers quickly, the telephone should be near the reference books that have brief answers. These have been discussed in the chapter 5. In a library with one telephone line, you may want to take the patron's name and number so that you can return the call rather than tying up the line. If you are alone in the library, you may be distracted by a patron, another telephone call, or any other matter. Returning the call is essential if good public relations are to be maintained.

More frequently, senior citizen centers are becoming outreach programs for local libraries. Providing books with large print, presenting book talks, and speaking with people there are fulfilling activities. Other outreach efforts, such as services to hospitals or inner city centers, are equally needed and also quite satisfying. Outreach services are limited only by the staff available to offer such services.

Loan of equipment to the community is another way to gain public approval of the library and its services. When a service organization or an association in the community wishes to have an audiovisual presentation but lacks equipment to use the materials, school and public libraries can provide this. Sometimes speakers come to a presentation but cannot carry the videotape recorder or overhead projector. When you can support such activities through the provision of equipment, the members of the service organization or the association will become advocates of the library.

Telefacsimile machines have become commonplace and are found in many libraries and in some homes. This facilitates the exchange of information from library to library in a way that was scarcely imagined only a short time ago. When you have access to a fax machine, it is much easier to provide copies of information from other locations, even from an international source, virtually instantaneously.

External services for interlibrary loan involve sending your materials when requested. When the request comes, you will be asked to prepare it for shipment, set the return date, and see that it is shipped. A carrier service may be specified, such as the post office or a commercial delivery system. Again, regulations for interlibrary loan are provided when you join the consortium or other partnership group.

You should prepare one or more presentations for organizations that invite you to speak. No better opportunity exists to present the library than a service organization interested in worthy causes. Presentations for community groups are effective methods of gaining library support. You may have to accept an invitation to present a program on a topic not necessarily library-oriented. However, you will use every opportunity to present the library to the community. If you are not comfortable with the prospect of making a presentation, read a book either from your library or another.

Collection-Related Services

These services include the following:

- Circulating materials

- Answering reference questions

- Adding to the collection

- Creating bibliographies

- Identifying special collections of patron interest

- Pulling in-depth research on a requested topic

As stated earlier, the collection-related services of circulation, reference, and adding to the collection are covered fully in chapters 4, 5, and 7 respectively, and will not be discussed at this time. They are listed here because you should consider the effects on other services of the time required to circulate materials, answer reference questions, and select new materials for your collection.

Providing bibliographies of information available in the library collection begins with a search of the card catalog or the online public access catalog for all materials available on a particular topic. The research and generation of copies may be much easier with an online public access catalog if you have subject search capability. Being able to generate bibliographies is one reason to ask a vendor for subject heading search capability when you establish the specifications for an online public access catalog.

Users may wish to have as much information on a topic as can possibly be found. When a patron solicits a bibliography of everything on a topic, the librarian gives as much help as possible in relation to other duties in the library. If the topic is a wide one, you may help the user narrow the search. This author well remembers the director of the National 4H Club program remarking about a request from a young 4H Club member who needed "everything you have on home economics." However, it is easier to update a bibliography once created than to begin at the beginning each time a request is made. If the request is one likely to be repeated soon, it is well worth the time to create a thorough bibliography.

One library task may be to identify special topics of interest and place them in a special location. For instance, many patrons read only one kind of book, such as westerns, science fiction, mysteries, or Victorian novels, among others. In a sense, a bibliography is created when these special topics are identified, marked, and placed in their own section of the library. You will quickly learn those topics that are frequently requested, and you can use this information to create unsolicited bibliographies. By placing these items in a single location, you save time over and over in finding these special collections for patrons. In contrast, you may merely create lists and keep them in a folder, hoping that, by having patrons look on the regular shelves for their choices, they may find a book of interest outside their more narrow topic.

Special topics may have seasonal interest, such as holiday books. Some librarians limit the use of holiday books to allow access by more patrons. Also, special topics may arise out of unusual occurrences, such as a coup in the former Soviet Union, that spur interest in the history of that country. A film shown on television or in the theaters will generate interest in the book that generated the movie.

Research collection or information gathering is a service of corporate librarians who are asked to locate information for their users and have it ready when sent for or when the user comes to get it. If you are working in a school library, you may be expected to collect all the material on a topic for a teacher to use in a class and place it on reserve or send it to the classroom on a book truck. If you are working in a public library, you may be more likely to help patrons locate materials immediately, rather than collecting information for someone who will appear later to collect it.

Youth Services in Public Libraries

Children's and young adult programming and services are provided in many public libraries. Such events are planned to attract audiences of children, all of whom have many other distractions and commitments. To do this effectively, you must become familiar with your collection as soon as possible. To answer the child who wants another book just like the last one or needs materials for a spider report, you must know what materials and what content are in the collection.

After offering programs, analyze the level of success to see if attendance merits similar programs in the future. Because children's and young adult programming and services may be a major assignment, this aspect of services is discussed in more detail here. Children's services include the following:

- Preschool story hours
- Reader's guidance
- Teaching library skills
- Storytelling
- Parenting activities
- Summer reading program
- Family literacy programs
- Children's book author and illustrator programs

Young adult programming includes the following:

- College information
- Study facilities
- Chess tournaments
- Job information

It is not easy to determine what types of programs to provide. In some states, the state library has a consultant assigned to work with public library programs for youth; this person will be helpful with suggestions for regular and special events. In other areas, regional library systems may have someone who can offer assistance. A review of current periodical literature by librarians working with these audiences will also suggest activities that have been well received. Only some beginning suggestions are made here for specific kinds of programming. It is also advisable to ⌂**Ask a Librarian**.

Programming for children includes both internal and external activities. Internal activities center on story hours throughout the year, parenting activities, storytelling, and the summer reading program. External activities include preschool story hours in day care centers.

Preschool story hours in day care centers can help introduce children to literature. Social service agencies have lists of day care centers. Go to the center in person, taking materials to leave for teachers. One of your assignments may be to encourage day care providers to share books with their children. When budget and collection permit, leave materials for children to take home for use there as well as while they are in the day care center.

Reader's guidance, almost the raison d'être for public and school libraries, includes helping children and young adults choose appropriate reading materials for pleasure and school work. You will be providing items at a level the child can read and understand, on a topic of interest, and, in the case of nonfiction books, on the topic of the child's research assignment. For adults, this may mean reading all the best-sellers so you can respond to "What's this all about?" In contrast, children are more likely to want a book "as good as this" (a difficult task if the reader has just finished *Homer Price* or *The Wind in the Willows*) or "another one by this author."

Reader's guidance also means book talks for older children, providing materials for book discussion groups, and book collections for classrooms, particularly for the whole language program. One aid to reader's guidance may mean collections of *genre books,* such as mystery and detective stories, science fiction, light romances, horse stories, or other items of special interest. It is much easier if you keep bibliographies of these repeatedly requested topics up-to-date to help locate all your materials, or you may mark the spine in some way for quick identification. Or, you may choose to place all genre books in special shelving. The argument for special shelving is the same for children as for adults. Science fiction fans might find another choice if the science fiction books were shelved among the rest of the fiction, but it is more likely they would leave in frustration at not finding any science fiction books.

The school librarian whose program is interrelated to the curriculum is likely to make teaching library skills a major focus. The basic task is to teach research skills and introduce information to students that they will use in conjunction with classroom lessons. This will be covered thoroughly later in this chapter. At the elementary level, school librarians introduce books to students through storytelling, and both elementary and secondary librarians share literature through book talks and reading aloud from books.

Teaching library skills is a formal requirement of school librarians, but it is also a part of the task of any public librarian. This service will be discussed in more detail later in the chapter.

Storytelling may be reading a book to children, showing them a film or filmstrip and playing a tape, or actually telling stories to preschool through primary grades. A list of books designed to improve storytelling skills and suggest books that lend themselves to being read or told is given in the annotated bibliography. Volunteers may be available to help with storytelling sessions if you are uncomfortable with this activity.

Story hours are offered throughout the year. During the day, programming is planned for an audience of preschool children. Schoolchildren may be attracted to Saturday sessions. Although story hours may be offered with stories read, children enjoy having stories told to them. Learning new stories for storytelling is time-consuming, and too often staff shortages limit the time that can be devoted to this. Plan picture books to read to children or show them the story on media. If you visit many preschools each week, it is unlikely you will have sufficient time to learn stories regularly. Planning story hours is an art. To seek further aid, ☐**Ask a Librarian**.

Youth librarians provide parenting activities designed to get mothers, fathers, and extended families actively involved in regular reading, so their children can observe the importance that adults attach to this skill. They are encouraged to demonstrate this importance by reading to their children and listening to children read aloud. If staff members are available, presentations for parents can be given when children are at story hour sessions. When staffing is limited, parents may be directed to a special display, handouts, and brochures in the story hour area. Whatever the time constraints, acknowledgment of the role of parents in family reading is a must.

The summer reading program is a major, essential effort to keep children reading throughout the summer months. This has been shown to be the most effective means of helping children retain their reading skills while school is out of session. Summer reading programs have a theme. Children are given an opportunity to read books and be recognized for their reading accomplishments. Prizes carrying out the theme are awarded for completing the program. If you need help in planning a summer reading program, ☐**Ask a Librarian**.

One of the most popular programs with children is an author or book illustrator visit. Local bookstores may help you arrange these. The author's availability may depend on your ability to pay for travel expenses. You also can order copies of books by the speaker for sale to the audience, with an autograph session following.

Many creative persons are reluctant to leave their workrooms, because this means time away from their creations. Author and illustrator visits may be shared with audiences from several schools or public libraries. The visit is carefully orchestrated to have as many children as possible meet the guest. Authors and illustrators are often good speakers with pleasant personalities. Such an event can be one of the most exciting happenings you can provide your patrons.

Young adult programming requires thorough analysis of the community, for the probable audience may be small. Teenagers are involved in school athletic teams, swimming, piano or dance lessons, social groups, and Senior Boy Scouts or Girl Scouts, with most activities taking precedence over a visit to the public library. Those who are not so busy with other activities may prefer to stay home and watch television. In contrast, some young adults use "going to the library, Mom," as an excuse to gain possession of an automobile for the evening. Their presence may not be welcomed by library staff. To plan a truly successful program for young adults, the subject of the program, the timing, and persons conducting sessions must be carefully selected. Publicity surrounding the event must be attractive and placed where many teens will see it, and evaluation of any program must be conducted to assess the success.

Young adults need information about colleges, so they can be encouraged to enroll. They and their parents must understand the offerings at the various institutions of higher education. Information about local community colleges, technical schools, and nearby universities, as well as information about schools nationwide will help students and parents who may be unfamiliar with how to choose a college or how to apply once the choice is made.

Providing study facilities at the public library may make it possible for a young adult to study. Many persons live in crowded conditions, with no quiet place to study. Further, many students are unable to get to the school library during the school day and need the resources of the local public library. Providing a study area away from other patrons may reduce the friction sometimes caused when teens do not behave exactly as adults might wish.

Chess tournaments are an example of the type of programming that may attract young adults to the public library. Just as articles in current library literature and books suggest activities to encourage younger children to use the library, such information is available to help you plan activities to encourage young adults to use the library. You must keep in mind also that young adults may wish to participate in some of the opportunities designed for your adult audience.

Adult Programming

Adult programming is touched on briefly here. Such programming could include the following:

- Book discussion groups
- Travelogues
- Information programs
- Literacy programs

There are formal book discussion groups such as the Great Books series. You can also encourage less formal sessions to discuss books. These involve each person reading the same book and arriving for a discussion. You may not have time to lead the discussion, but you will be involved in providing copies of the books to be discussed, and you may be asked to suggest books that would be of interest to the group.

Travelogues are another popular event that can be exciting for both participants and speakers. Those who travel enjoy sharing their experiences with others, and these can be excellent programs if the presenters have accurate and broad knowledge about the places, buildings, culture, and other facts beyond what someone might learn from a tour guide. These presenters should confirm that slides are in order, that there are many different views rather than repetitive shots of a single spot, and that slides are presented slowly enough for the audience to appreciate, but not so long as to become boring. In this way, members of the community can share their trips and provide good programming.

Many persons have video cameras that can tell the tale if the camera person added a good narrative while filming or later, though this skill is not often seen in many home videos. Audiences accustomed to quality documentaries such as those on television might embarrass an inexpert presenter in your library.

You can identify information programs that will be interesting and beneficial to your clientele. These may range from tax experts talking about preparing tax forms to extension agents who discuss weed killers for flower beds, to fashion experts or poets reading their work, among others. Voter information is also important, and you will walk a narrow line between providing information and endorsing a candidate.

Your patrons may enjoy programs that allow them to participate actively. Among these are book discussion programs and chess tournaments that may be regular or irregular, arts or crafts demonstrations, among others.

Perhaps the most active participation can come from literacy programs. Many literacy programs, though not administered by the local public library, are housed there. As discussed earlier, the library is an acceptable location for an adult to go, and the stigma placed on going to school is not given to going to the library. If your library is a site for literacy volunteer tutors and their students, provide a pleasant room and privacy.

These divisions or categories of services do not stand alone but are integrally related. Programming may be offered outside the library, using information gathered from the collection. In this context, "programming" is a means of enticing clientele into your library, introducing them to the contents of your collection, helping them expand their uses of information, and building an affirmative perception of information services.

This list of services is limited in comparison to the variety discussed in the literature and presented at meetings of librarians and information professionals. However, it can give you a general idea of types of services offered by libraries.

COSTING OUT SERVICES

Once you have identified the services you presently offer and determine what services you would like to add, you need to analyze the cost-effectiveness of your present services. As you find out which services are actually used and appreciated by patrons, you will begin to understand where your priorities for service lie. If a service is seldom used, little of your time should be allocated to it. Analyzing what services actually cost can help you decide which to expand, which to reduce, and which to maintain at the current level, based on their cost-effectiveness. If you feel a less used but important service is cost effective, you will need to target it for selling to your users.

DECISION TWO: What services should be offered?

Determine what each service offered actually costs the library. The model shown in tables 6.1 and 6.2 may help you analyze current services based on a cost analysis of their effectiveness. For this exercise, costs are calculated in simple rounded figures, with little if any relationship to the real world.

Utilities/upkeep at library at $200 per 10-hour day or $20 per hour

Professional staff time is $10 per hour

Clerical staff time at $5 per hour

Books cost $10, periodicals $10 per year, media $10 per item

What do the services in the "Need" column cost per month?

Table 6.1.

Audience (10,000 in community)	Need	Staff	Facility	Time	Budget	Evaluation	Dissemination
25 users	interlibrary loan	1 prof	computer mailing	6 hrs	$60 $60	oral	report to bd
800 children	40 day care centers	1 prof	out of bldg	80 hrs bks	$800 $200	oral	news rpt to bd
1,000	ready reference	1 prof	tele ref/col	50 hrs bks	$500 $100	none	bd rpt
25 users	research	1 prof	ref/col bks	25 hrs	$250 $500	oral	bd rpt

To move this to a yearly amount: Total Budget: $30,000

Table 6.2.

	#users/%	Budget Amount		% of budget
i.l.l.	25/.25%	$120 per month x 12 =	$ 1,440	4.8%
day care	800/8%	$1,000 per month x 12 =	12,000	40%
ready ref.	1000/10%	$600 per month x 12 =	7,200	24%
research	25/.25%	$750 per month x 12 =	6,000	20%
		Total	$26,540	

ACTION ONE: Determine the quality of services.

Assess quality by the responses to the evaluation questions as indicated, including the percentage using the service, how often they are using the service, and their level of satisfaction.

- What percentage of patrons use the service?

In our simple example in tables 6.1 and 6.2, you have a very expensive service in "research," for you have 20 percent of your budget allocated to only .25 percent of your users.

- How often are patrons using the service?

Again, if you compare reference hours, you find that professional staff is spending 25 hours with 25 users doing research, and only 50 hours with 1,000 users on "ready reference."

- What level of satisfaction do users assign to this service?

For the sake of this example, let us say that everyone is pleased with their service.

ACTION TWO: Determine the need for the service.

- If the service were discontinued, who would complain?

You must always consider that not everyone can complain if a service is discontinued. Certainly, it would be difficult for day care children to launch any type of organized reaction to cutting their story hours. Also, because some ready reference is by telephone, infrequent callers might not understand that there is now a wait before calls are answered or that the service is not available during certain hours.

- If the service were reduced, who would complain?

The same arguments prevail here as for the first question.

- If the service were expanded, what would it take?

This can be calculated by determining the additional hours and placing them in the matrix.

A method for clientele, governing boards, or individuals to rank services is suggested in chapter 8. However, based on all of the above information, you could assign a priority ranking to each service for continuing at the same level, increasing the service, decreasing, or deleting it.

WHAT WILL NEW SERVICES PROVIDE?

After your thorough analysis of present services, you now turn to adding services. Programming for latchkey children, database searching, a film program, preparing students for a statewide storytelling contest, and having tax expertise available in the library will be used as generic examples, again using the sample costs used earlier.

Some community leaders have noted the problem of latchkey children who need some place to wait, one or more days each week, until an adult arrives at home. Even if no program is provided, these children will add a cost to library service in clerical monitoring of volunteers and addition of materials to the collection. How would adding formal library services for latchkey children affect the staff and the functioning of your library, and how might it be possible to minimize disruption?

Fifth-grade students wish to prepare for a statewide storytelling contest. Teachers and the school librarian bring the children to the library auditorium to videotape their performances. The storytelling contest each year depletes the school's collection, so students and their parents often come to your library to find stories to tell.

You have surveyed your community and found that adults need income tax assistance. The local Internal Revenue Service office has trained students from a nearby law school to offer assistance. You need to provide space for four weeks in late March and early April for them to consult with adults in the community. You anticipate that 200 persons will make use of this service.

Objective One: To provide reference, tutoring, and recreation for 30 children after school, 2 hours per day, 5 days per week, 40 hours per month for 10 months = 400 in-library hours.

Objective Two: To provide an opportunity for 300 fifth-grade students to prepare for their annual storytelling contest. This will take five minutes per student (1,500 minutes or 25 hours).

Objective Three: To provide income tax assistance to 200 persons in the community, using volunteers from the local law school. This will require an anticipated 100 hours total use, but you will plan for more than one volunteer in the library. This means you must set aside more than one room during the time the volunteers are in the building.

For each objective, the cost in staff time, the "reservations" for rooms in the library, and the time allocated to staff and rooms that is required is detailed. Any costs in miscellaneous materials is noted. As is shown in the previous table, dissemination of the outcome in terms of success is outlined.

Table 6.3.

Audience (10,000 in community)	Need	Staff	Facility	Time	Budget	Evaluation	Dissemination
30 latch-key children	volunteers materials	1 clerk	1 room	40 hrs 40 hrs	$200 $800 $400	none	rpt to board
300 students	25 tapes	1 clerk	camera auditorium	25 hrs 25 hrs	$125 $ 75 $500	# winners	news rpt to bd
200 adults	volunteers		2 rooms	100 hrs	$2000	oral	news rpt to bd

Your yearly cost for the programs above is:

Latchkey children @ $1,400 per month for 10 months	$14,000
Story tapes @ $700 for one month	$700
Income tax program for one month	$2,000
Total	$16,700

You have identified new services you wish to offer, and you have analyzed each service in terms of the probable audience, confirming how it will meet a need and how it will affect staff and facility; materials and equipment needed as available or to be purchased; time required; and probable costs. You must now determine how these changes will affect present services.

In planning your original services, you had $30,000 in your budget, of which you expended $26,540, leaving $3,460. The total anticipated cost of new programs is $16,700, giving you a shortfall of over $16,000, if no cost for any service exceeds what you have budgeted.

If you are going to offer the new services, you will need to do the following:

- Reduce or eliminate some old services

- Reduce or eliminate some new services

- Seek additional funding

- All of the above

This information is used to assess the impact on the current budget, to explain to administrators the implications and the need for the service, and to explain to administrators the need for additional funding.

If the budget remains the same, a decision must be made to either cut an existing service or to delay adding the new service. Reallocation of funds from the reference department could provide the new service at the "expense" of cutting telephone reference services on weekends. How this would affect patrons must be weighed carefully against the need for the new service.

TEACHING IN THE LIBRARY

Behavior of users sets the climate for your library. Obviously, behavior is more focused in a school library than in a public library, because students are regularly in school. Patrons in a public library who cause problems are removed by law enforcement officers.

Library Citizenship

Library users need to understand that the library and its contents belong to them, and they should take care of materials because they do "own" them. This is demonstrated by the attitudes of staff who welcome users and offer them as many materials as possible to fulfill their needs. As discussed under staffing in chapter 3, a welcome atmosphere creates the forum for good library citizenship and the concept of sharing among patrons completes this process.

From their first visits to the library, children are taught how to care for the materials in the library. How to open books, how to place microcomputer disks into the disk drive, how to keep all such items out of the way of younger brothers and sisters are first lessons.

Library citizenship for adults includes everything from gentle reminders that others may need materials that are due back in the library to asking authorities to remove an inebriated person from the outside steps. Overdue materials are a problem for all libraries, but sending the sheriff may get the book back at a great loss of good feelings about the library. The dilemma of problem patrons is one that is difficult to solve in any library, but patrons should have as much freedom as possible as long as they are not disturbing others.

Teaching Library Skills

If users are to become familiar with services offered, including arrangement of materials and equipment, rules for using materials, and holdings of the library, the easiest method is to teach this use in a regular manner. In the school, this may be accomplished by conducting formal classes. In both school and public libraries, training is reinforced by preparing self-instruction modules for individualized instruction and by placing instructions on posters and signs.

Learning cannot occur without immediate application. Practice makes perfect. Teaching a skill that will not be practiced immediately is a waste of time for both teacher and designated learner.

Many materials have been prepared to help you teach library skills. Please refer to the bibliography for a list of some to help you begin, or you may **Ask a Librarian**.

When adults have been library users for a long time, the only skills they may need to be taught are those related to new technologies that provide access to information. User-friendly computer programs make it possible to use online public access catalogs with little instruction.

GLOSSARY

Genre books. Specialized fiction books such as westerns, mysteries, science fiction, and romances that have similar themes.

Chapter 7

ADDING TO
THE COLLECTION

Because your library is a first source of information for your regular clientele, your collection must be adequate to meet their needs. That is, materials must be relevant, up-to-date, and in sufficient quantities to answer the information questions asked by patrons and to provide the resources needed for their research projects. Adding regularly to your collection is the best way to provide appropriate materials for ever-changing user requests. This chapter discusses adding to the collection, establishing needs, writing a collection development plan, selecting and acquiring materials and equipment, processing them for use, and the relationship of the budget to this process.

Collection development is a continuing assignment for you and your staff as you manage your library. The process is facilitated when a selection policy is in place. Collection development begins with the application of criteria published in your selection policy.

SETTING THE STAGE:
THE SELECTION POLICY

A selection policy describes the process used to evaluate materials for inclusion in the library collection. You develop criteria to apply to each item before adding it to your collection, thus insuring a quality collection that supports the needs of users.

Selection policies may be required for information agencies that are tax supported and have patrons from the public at large, such as school and public libraries. Whether or not such a document is required, you should develop your own. Your policy accomplishes the following:

- It interprets the selection process for administrators, staff, and users.

- It confirms your choices when you purchase new materials.

- It provides a method to meet challenges to items in the collection, items being ordered for the collection, and items being offered to the library by outside groups.

- It justifies the removal of items no longer useful to users.

The selection policy is used to answer all questions concerning materials that may be sensitive to one or more groups, and it helps explain the disposition of all donations. This policy confirms when materials will no longer be retained in the collection.

Your document may begin with a global statement of purpose applicable to all library collections. Selection policies should also include the following:

- Designation of the governing body responsible for the collection and a statement of philosophy of this body concerning materials and intellectual freedom

- Aims and objectives of the library, and the relationship of the collection to the objectives of the library and the philosophy of the governing body

- A list of persons, titles, or positions of your selection committee or a list of all who participate in reviewing selection policies, in implementing policies, and in selecting materials

- Names or titles of persons with final authority for selection

- General criteria to be applied to items considered for purchase

- Selection aids frequently used, preview policies, and specific criteria applied to the selection of special collections, e.g., local history materials

- Examples of forms used to record suggested purchases, with procedures for ranking or prioritizing purchases

- Policies toward gifts, deselection, duplication, and replacement

- Cooperative acquisition programs, networking arrangements, among others

- Instructions for handling complaints

Designation of Governing Body

Libraries are the responsibility of a wide variety of governing bodies. "Governing body" for your selection policy will be the group that endorses the policy. In the case of public and school libraries, these are the public library board and the school board. For your policy to be legal, it must be officially approved by such individuals.

Objectives of the Collection

Not all agencies have published aims or a philosophy. Nevertheless, you should develop objectives for your collection that place it within the central functions of the agency. A school library is an integral part of the educational mission of the school. A public library is an integral part of service to the community. Agencies need information that is provided by their special libraries. Whether or not a central mission statement exists for your agency, your objectives should support the raison d'être for activities of clientele within that agency.

Selection Committee

You may have in place either a formal or an informal selection process or both. Such a process helps you develop the collection plan, from prioritizing purchases to placing new items on the shelves. The more formal process would involve a selection committee to provide wider participation in the selection process. Committee members

- attend selection meetings,
- participate in establishing the collection development plan,
- assist in the preview and review of items for the collection,
- record opinions about the quality of any item being considered for purchase, and
- help prioritize purchases.

The selection committee is made up of staff, users, and others with interest in the collection. Members are chosen to get wide representation of potential and actual users. They will be directly involved in the review and preview process by reviewing materials and analyzing the evaluation forms submitted by others.

You should be the final authority in the selection process because you will understand user needs and budget constraints. If your operation is large enough to merit an acquisitions person, this person may also be listed as having authority for approving purchase orders. Such arrangements will be described in job descriptions as well as designated in the selection policy.

Selection Criteria

Selection criteria for the addition of materials to any collection will include general considerations such as the following:

- Authenticity

Authentic material is described as accurate, up-to-date, free from bias or prejudice. This may be prejudged by the reputation of the author or producer. Reviews of items in professional publications will also discuss some of these points. Obviously, an in-house preview is needed for final confirmation.

- Use

Items should be judged on whether they will be used. That is, will the item stimulate interest and provide information that is needed by users?

- Content

An item may be considered high-quality by all who have reviewed it in the literature or even by your evaluation committee. Yet, the content of this new item may be on a topic that is well covered in the collection and information is more critically needed on other subjects. Therefore, the item may be cited for purchase, but it should not be given a high priority for purchase.

- Technical qualities

Technical qualities more often apply to media than to books, although books should be well-bound in good paper. Technical qualities as applied to audiovisual media include effective photography, readable captions, excellent soundtrack, and well-written narrative. Voice quality of the narrator will also be a consideration, because listeners prefer a pleasant voice.

- Relevance

Information should have relevance to the user. That is, it should be timely. "Antique" information may be misinformation.

Final, overall criteria may include the following:

- Is the item worth the price?

- Is it significant?

- Does it promise longevity of appeal and interest?

- Are any accompanying guides available, and, if so, are they well-written, containing helpful information beyond a description of the product?

The remainder of the items suggested for inclusion in your selection policy—selection aids, policies toward gifts, cooperative acquisition programs and networking, and intellectual freedom issues—will be covered in depth later in this chapter.

Once the draft selection policy has been written, it should be given to the governing body for approval. In the case of school or public libraries, this is the board of education or the public library board. Their acceptance of the document removes its "draft" designation. Other agencies may not require such formal review; yet a selection policy is needed to help with difficult selection decisions.

Selection policies should be carefully constructed to include the necessary general coverage of selection processes. Because they must be approved by others, it is not a good idea to have them under regular revision. Rather, your selection policy should have broad general applications and address process rather than the nitty-gritty of procedures of acquiring materials from suppliers.

ESTABLISHING COLLECTION NEEDS

To select items for your collection that are based on user needs, you must learn what is presently available in your library. Then you test the collection to see how well it matches the needs of users. Three testing methods are suggested. Others may be found in the annotated bibliography.

1. Use circulation information.

Circulation information may become a basis for establishing which areas or items of the collection are heavily used. However, circulation statistics will not tell you what materials are actually being used and how well the information is serving the needs of patrons. Further, circulation numbers do not provide information regarding in-house use of the library. To evaluate user satisfaction, you must survey users.

2. Ask for input from users.

Some users will complain if they cannot find the information they need. Others may just leave and do without the information or go elsewhere for their needs. When no one states satisfaction with or complaints against the information available, you may need to conduct some fact-finding studies. Figure 7.1 is a simple form that can be used to identify user needs.

```
Name_____
Location_____  Phone _____
I need information on the following: By (date):


This information will be used for:
          presentation
          report
          other:


I prefer _____ books _____ magazine articles, etc.

```

Fig. 7.1. Form to identify user needs.

Users can also evaluate their degree of satisfaction with the information they have found or that you have provided for them. Formal evaluation mechanisms will be discussed in chapter 8. However, informal discussions with users can help identify some collection gaps. If you ask users in the library if they found what they needed, if it was relevant, accurate, and sufficient, you can record the negative responses and suggest those to the selection committee for priority purchases.

3. Analyze the collection.

Collections age and some items become less useful for many reasons, including new discoveries of all types, from new planets and stars to new medications. Countries are given new names, changing references to people and places. Also, materials may sit unused when they are no longer best-sellers. Fad literature in a particular field, such as *Cultural Literacy* or *Future Shock,* is replaced by new books by previous authors, new authors, new directions, or new information. Patron interests may change as communities get new residents or schools adopt new curricula. Once you have determined the areas of largest circulation, identified the stated needs of users, and reviewed the collection, you will write a collection development plan.

COLLECTION DEVELOPMENT PLANS

A collection development plan differs from a selection policy in the following ways:

- It need not be formally approved.

This document is developed in consultation with your selection committee and reflects the current state of your collection. It is your plan to emphasize certain topics when you begin preparing orders for new materials.

- It is under constant scrutiny.

Specific areas of the collection are emphasized when a new or increased need is established. You identify areas of the collection that should be targeted or areas that need special attention because of new circumstances. These become high priorities for the budget process. An example would be a special clientele such as a growing population of senior citizens with vision problems, who would require more large-print books. Special education students might be mainstreamed, indicating new purchases. Gifted or honors program students might need special information.

- It is brief.

Although it may be a written document, it can also be an outline, or it may be simply the placement of order cards in priority order. It could also be a notebook with wish lists justified by a needs assessment.

Your collection development plan will help you when budgets are given, for you will be able to make a careful distribution rather than basing selection decisions on the most recent complaint about lack of information.

The plan is updated as new needs are identified. As you find patrons using out-of-date information because it is all that can be found on the shelf, you can begin to locate replacement titles. You will want to make sure your collection does not give users misinformation.

Once your collection plan has identified the areas of need for materials, you are ready to begin your search for items to meet those needs. You may find that few patrons have specific items in mind for you to purchase. Keeping a supply of order cards on the front of the chargeout desk will remind patrons that you are interested in their suggestions. However, you may need to rely on other means for selecting new materials.

SELECTING MATERIALS
FOR THE COLLECTION

Choosing materials for any library collection is one of the more pleasant tasks. Identifying what patrons need and what is available from vendors provides you an opportunity to meet with users, to visit trade shows, to attend professional association meetings, and to preview items. For those who must miss some of those opportunities, using selection aids, including reviews in the literature, becomes a substitute.

Selection Aids

Help is available as you begin to locate materials for purchase. For those unable to view collection items at trade shows, some substitutes provide opportunities to locate quality materials. You may find a suggested list of basic materials deemed necessary for a certain kind of library. This is called a core collection. Such lists can more often be found for selecting materials for school and public libraries. The core collection is one individual's or a group of individuals' opinion of what is needed. It may or may not meet the needs of your patrons. However, such a list is a good starting place, and it is sometimes useful in deciding what volumes to weed from a collection. Some examples of these basic lists that are selection tools include

- *Children's Catalog, Junior High Catalog, High School Catalog.* These three buying guides list best collections for children through high school and are published by the H. W. Wilson Company. Annual paperback supplements are published in hard cover every five years. Entries are chosen by a committee of librarians, which selects the best in-print fiction and nonfiction. Books and brief annotations are listed in Dewey Classification order, fiction, and easy fiction. An author, title, and subject index are included.

- *Public Library Catalog.* Another selection tool from H. W. Wilson, this recommended list is designed for public librarians. Entries are chosen by a committee of librarians.

- Gillespie, John. *Best Books for Children: Preschool through Grade 6.* 4th ed. New York: R. R. Bowker, 1990. $48.00. All books have been recommended in at least three review journals. Each entry has bibliographic data and a brief annotation with grade level. Source of recommendation is also given. This is helpful as justification for any purchase that may be under a censorship attack.

- *Reference Books Bulletin.* Chicago: American Library Association. This publication includes all reviews from *Reference Books Bulletin* within the indicated dates. They are arranged under format (bibliographies, dictionaries, encyclopedias, etc.) alphabetically by title. Reviews of online reference tools and works appearing only in microform are included.

The above are but a small sample of many of the evaluation tools available. Some are chosen by committees of librarians, others by professional reviewers, and still others are collections of reviews from other sources, particularly reviews from reviewing journals.

Journals and library periodicals review materials for libraries. These include general professional periodicals, professional association periodicals, and reviewing services:

- General professional periodicals

  Library Journal
  School Library Journal
  Public Library Quarterly

- Professional association periodicals

  American Libraries
  School Library Media Quarterly

- Reviewing services

  Booklist
  Kirkus

Most of these periodicals review materials of high interest to school or public librarians. *Booklist* and *Kirkus* are reviewing periodicals with little other information, and the professional periodicals and professional association periodicals have articles, job opportunities, and other information of interest to librarians.

Review and Preview

Although many aids to selection are available, you should actually review or preview items whenever possible. By seeing materials before purchase, you can match the contents of potential purchases to the actual needs of your users in relation to what you already have in your collection. Specific and more detailed information is not available in the brief annotations of most review journals or recommended lists. You will especially want to preview any items that take a substantial portion of your collection budget.

DECISION ONE: To preview materials before purchase.

Previewing items before ordering helps you and your selection committee understand the content of items, including how much information is given, the accuracy and relevancy of the information, the vocabulary or level of difficulty, and the possible interest of any user in the information.

ACTION ONE: Establish a preview request system.

To maintain an orderly process, establish a preview system. Staff or patrons request materials to be considered for purchase, review, and recommendation for purchase. Even though an item is not deemed suitable or a priority to purchase, the preview file will help remind you that you have previously previewed the item. The first step is to decide what will happen to an item requested for preview.

ACTION TWO: Order for preview.

1. Identify items to be previewed.

Items may be found in review periodicals or at conferences, or they may be requested by users. A form such as the one in figure 7.2 may be used to record requests.

Please send the following item for preview (author, title, date, publisher/producer with address):

Previewed by: Recommended by:

Disposition:

Item in collection under call number:

Item ordered: (date)

Item to be ordered as funds are available:

Item not ordered. Similar item presently available in collection is:

Fig. 7.2. Form for recording requests for preview items.

You maintain a list of previewed materials to prevent inadvertently ordering a previously previewed item. The record is maintained even though the item is not judged to be acceptable for purchase.

2. Request materials from the producer.

3. Persons who requested the item for preview are invited to see the item, or sent the item to preview.

4. Post lists of items received for preview to see if others are interested in previewing them.

5. Previewers complete evaluation forms.
Sample evaluation forms may be found in the books listed in the annotated bibliography.

6. Items are then returned to the producer or supplier before the due dates.

ACTION THREE: Establish a potential order file.

Based on the outcome of the preview process, you build a potential order file. This file will help you make quality purchases when either expected or unexpected funds are available to purchase. Additions are made to this order file

- as materials are previewed, using the preview process and based on the priorities established by the selection committee;

- from recommendations in selection aids and periodical reviews; and

- from user suggestions.

One word of caution: Before adding any item to the potential order file (and again before an order is given to a supplier), determine if you already own the material. Unnecessary, unwanted duplication of purchases is a double cost, for you have something you do not need, and you cannot purchase another item that you do need. To minimize this happening, you should check the following:

- Your card catalog or online public access catalog to see if you already own an item

- Your order file to see if it is on order

- Your potential order file to see if it is a high priority purchase

- Your preview request file to see if it was previewed but not given a high rating by reviewers. This may confirm why it was not purchased previously.

In addition, you may want to check your shelflist to see the number and quality of items in your collection on this topic or by this author, in case this might not be a priority purchase at present.

ACQUIRING MATERIALS

You have a prioritized potential purchase order file that has been checked to see that items are not currently in the collection. You are now ready to place an order. You will need to know the cost of items, so that you order within your established budget allocation. Several reference tools are available with up-to-date information on the published cost of items:

Books in Print. New York: R. R. Bowker. Annual. Lists every book in print in the United States with author, title, publisher, and price. This is also available on CD-ROM.

Children's Books in Print. New York: R. R. Bowker, 1969—. Annual. $139.00. Titles for children.

The IMS/Ayer Directory of Publications. Guide to newspapers, newsletters, and serials that are published at least five times a year.

Paperback Books in Print. New York: R. R. Bowker. Annual (at the public library, on CD-ROM, at the local college).

Subject Guide to Books in Print. New York: R. R. Bowker. Annual. A companion volume to *Books in Print*, this reference lists books by subject.

Subject Guide to Children's Books in Print. New York: R. R. Bowker, 1970—. Annual. $139.00. A subject listing of children's books in print.

Ulrich's International Periodicals Directory. This guide to periodicals is arranged by subject, with buying information.

All of the above are helpful in establishing the cost of items. You may find that the published cost and the real cost are not the same. Most librarians are given a discount on orders, based on the size of the order. As the number of items purchased increases, the discount given for each item increases. For this reason, many smaller libraries band together to order materials to increase their volume of purchases and thus maximize any discounts provided by suppliers.

Negotiating for a discount means that you tell the supplier the number of items being purchased each year or the probable amount of funds to be allocated for purchases from that vendor. Through personal contacts with vendors, you may convince the company that you should have a better discount than is published.

One choice may be to send smaller orders to individual publishers, thereby increasing your discount but also increasing your paperwork. You may choose to order from a jobber who represents many publishers. Jobbers have a variety of means for ordering, from typing a purchase order to ordering electronically. Many jobbers now provide processing for the materials they supply. Processed materials are discussed below.

Some agencies require advertising for bids. This means that a list of what you plan to purchase is sent to possible vendors, and they submit an amount that they are willing to accept in exchange for the items listed. If your agency requires bids for items, check to see if this includes all items, purchases under a certain amount (such as $100), or certain items, but not all. You also need to understand the process thoroughly, so that your specifications for items insure that you receive quality products rather than what a low bid vendor can give you. Low bids for poorly described items can mean inferior merchandise.

Your agency will have a procedure in place for placing orders. This process should be described in your procedures manual. If not, you need to write a careful description of the steps to follow, after consulting with an accounting person. Special forms may be required, and a signature other than your own may be needed before any item may be purchased.

You also need to know the amount of time it takes for such a process to be carried out. The time of year that an item is ordered and delivered may mean that the item is ordered in one budget year but delivered in the next. This is a double loss to your budget, for you have "lost" the money from the past year because you did not receive an item for that amount. Also, you will now be charged for that item in the second year, and that means you will be unable to order as much as you thought your budget would cover for the new year.

You may choose to order from a wide variety of sources. Certainly some librarians have ordering needs as complicated or even more complicated than those of other departments in their agency. If your orders are sent out through a central purchasing office, staff there may be reluctant to place orders for small amounts, because the processing of the order is more costly than the item purchased.

You can place a standing order to a vendor. That is, you wish to receive all the materials published on a certain topic. You will purchase these sight unseen rather than wait until reviews are available or you receive notice of publication from another source. You will need to work out the details with the individual vendor to assure the mechanism for receiving and billing for these materials.

Shipments arrive and contents are matched to the order forms to insure that the items ordered are the items received. As soon as any order is received, the billing for that order is matched to the items received, so that a check may be sent. A vendor who ships a partial order of books is paid in two installments, or you may decide to hold payment on a system until all components are shipped, installed, and working.

PROCESSING MATERIALS

Processing materials includes cataloging—preparing a record for the user to find the new items in the collection—and preparing materials for use. If your library still has a card catalog, you should purchase preprocessed materials whenever you can. This means the item arrives with catalog cards, spine markings, pockets, and circulation cards. Cataloging information on preprocessed materials may not be satisfactory to every cataloger, but it should be accurate enough that your users can find the items. It is a well-known axiom that seven catalogers would catalog seven items in seven different ways. Questioning the cataloging output of your reputable supplier will be more time-consuming, especially if you must re-catalog and create cards or make data entry for your OPAC.

Cataloging Items

Items that are not ready for the shelves will require some form of description or cataloging. You may decide that some simple record will be sufficient. Such a system may be adequate for you, but you must consider what happens when you move to another position.

As mentioned earlier, a classification scheme should be chosen. To do original cataloging requires a professional. Please ▢**Ask a Librarian** to help you understand this process.

One help for persons with little cataloging experience has been the *cataloging in publication (CIP)* provided on the back of the title page of many books. CIP provides cataloging information, including subject headings.

In chapter 5, on references, access points to the collection were mentioned. Access points will be by author, first word of the title, and assigned subject headings. As discussed in chapter 1, subject headings will lead users to the items listed as having information on that subject.

Preparing Materials for Use

After materials have been cataloged, they must be made shelf-ready. For books and other items that circulate, this means attaching a bar code, if you have an automated system, or a pocket and card if you have a manual system. Plastic jackets may be placed on books that have book jackets. Some persons laminate the covers of paperback books to extend their life. Such systems can be demonstrated by the vendors selling the products to do this task.

Vertical file materials are dated so that their age can be easily determined. Subjects should be identified in a central spot on each item, so that items can be returned to file folders when users have returned them to you.

Periodicals may be stored using many different methods. You must decide how you wish to store your periodicals.

DECISION TWO: How to store periodicals.

Publishers give each magazine an issue number and a volume number. If a periodical is published each month, issue one would be January. If the periodical has been published for 10 years, the next January will be issue one, volume 11. Because publishers number their periodicals in chronological order, you should store them in this order for easy retrieval. They may be stored in one of the following ways:

- Stacked on open shelves
- Placed in boxes called "Princeton Files"
- Bound together
- On microfilm

Maintaining the correct chronological order of single copies of periodicals requires a great deal of attention. It is sometimes impossible to keep them on open shelves because users seldom replace issues where they belong. Furthermore, it is easy for a patron to carry away a single issue, making your "run" (all the issues in any volume) incomplete. However, if you follow the policy of keeping back issues only for five years, this is a problem that resolves itself.

By contrast, bound volumes are easier to store and remain in order; however, they present a few problems. These can be used by only one person at a time. It is more difficult to make a copy of an article if it has been placed in a hard binding. Also, although pages may be ripped out and articles cut from any magazine, it seems more horrifying when issues are bound. Sending volumes to the bindery means they are out of circulation while they are there. Further, binding is costly unless you have binding capability in your agency.

One solution to the storage of periodicals is to purchase microfiche of back issues or have periodicals microfilmed. This provides efficient storage; however, most patrons will prefer hard copy to microfilm. Another solution is to buy full text CD-ROM products.

Nonprint materials often require special shelving, especially when facilities are small and shelving is limited. For instance, it would take a box the size of a book to house a single filmstrip to be shelved with the other items on a topic. Also, some items such as videotapes, audiocassettes, and CDs may appear too costly to place on open shelves. The dust jacket is placed on the open shelves for patrons to see what is available, but they must ask at the desk for the actual item. If you decide to have all materials integrated on your shelves, you will need to choose suitable containers for nonprint items.

Filing Cards in the Card Catalog

As stated in chapter 5, it is important that you choose a filing system and use it at all times for placing cards in the card catalog. Obviously if you have an online public access catalog, filing of entries is automatic. However, if you have a card catalog, cards must be filed using a filing system. If you are the only person working in your information center, you should file cards above the rod and leave them for a short time. This will allow you a second look before you drop the cards permanently into the drawer. If you have assistants doing filing, ask them to leave the cards above the rod until you can review their work.

DESELECTING MATERIALS (WEEDING)

As much as you may wish to keep everything forever, items wear out, get out of date, or are replaced by new information. Few items in any library are classics, and little-used, outdated, worn-out items must be reviewed. The process for deselecting materials follows the pattern for selection, in that criteria for placement in your library are applied, and if the item is no longer needed, relevant, or in good condition, all records of its being in the library are removed. Also, items that are permanently borrowed (stolen) by anonymous users must also be deleted from your collection.

Cards are pulled from the card catalog or items deleted from the database when the item has been deselected. For both card catalog and database, the process of removal is walking backward along the same path as preparing entries originally. You must pull all the cards or records that were filed for each item. This process is easy when a record is maintained on main entry-author cards and shelflist cards. This record indicates the other cards prepared, such as joint author or editor, illustrator, and subject headings, among others. One of the reasons that system designers suggest that any collection be thoroughly weeded before establishing an electronic database is that it is as difficult if not more difficult to remove a record from an electronic file than to input that record. This is even more difficult when the record is added to a CD-ROM file.

Whatever the effort involved, when an item is deleted from the collection, all records of that item must be removed, including items on bibliographies you have generated. If this is not done, patrons will be unhappy when they turn up a promising citation only to find that the item is no longer in the collection.

If the topic of a deselected item is important, a replacement is ordered. An item in poor condition may still be needed, and, if it is still in print, a duplicate copy is ordered. Many books have chapters on weeding the library collection. See the annotated bibliography for assistance.

One final deselection process involves deleting records for items that have been lost or stolen. Librarians may choose to wait for one or more years in case an item is returned. You must decide whether it is more trouble to tell patrons that an item listed in your card catalog or OPAC is lost than it would be to re-enter the item if it is returned after some time.

SELECTING EQUIPMENT

When equipment selection and purchase are assigned to the librarian, the process is not included in selection policy for books and media. Rather, equipment purchase follows choice of media formats. Obviously users will need equipment required for items requiring accompanying equipment. Equipment is not itself an information source, but a platform for the information.

Information about quality of equipment is not as easily located as recommended lists for books and other media. However, some sources that should be helpful are included in the annotated bibliography.

Criteria for the evaluation of equipment will include such characteristics as the following:

- Ease of operation

Equipment that is complicated to operate will daunt all but the most aggressive of technology users. You and your patrons must operate any piece of equipment regularly to remain knowledgeable about and comfortable with its operation. The more difficult that machinery is to run, the more likely that it will not function smoothly, thus discouraging further use.

- User friendliness

You should provide complete, simple operating instructions with diagrams for all pieces of equipment, so that users find the process friendly. If not, they will become frustrated and give up even though actual operation is quite easy. Perhaps the most important instruction is to remind users that all equipment using electricity should be plugged into an outlet.

- Availability for technology tests

Vendors should make their equipment available for demonstration and testing in your library. Just having a salesperson come and demonstrate is not enough. Obviously company representatives know how to operate their products, but will you or your users? Time to test the equipment will also allow you an opportunity to see how much instruction you, your staff, and your users will need to begin to use the equipment. Vendors who are unwilling to allow you to test their equipment may be afraid that you will discover its obvious shortcomings.

- Ease of repair and maintenance

All equipment is kept in top-notch running order. If you have a piece of equipment that is not functioning properly, users will think they cannot operate it. Nothing is as frustrating as hoping to view a videotape or listen to a tape and being unable to do so because the equipment is malfunctioning. Therefore, in considering what kind of equipment to purchase, you should consider how to have it inspected regularly and how to get it repaired when it does not work.

You will need to keep a record of repairs made on each piece of equipment. When the amount spent to repair any item in a year exceeds the purchase price for a new item, new equipment should be purchased.

- Anticipated life

You should estimate the probable life of any piece of equipment, so a budget item can be set aside for its replacement at the appropriate time. Your choice of brand purchased will depend on the quality of each product and how long each will be expected to operate before major repairs are needed or before it wears out entirely.

- Compatibility

Often, manufacturers produce equipment from technology that is incompatible with that of another manufacturer. Examples of this are the videocassette recorder and microcomputer markets. Initially, in the VCR market, it was a battle between BetaMax technology and VHS technology. Today's microcomputer market is divided between IBM-style PCs and Macintoshes. Each uses different operating systems and software programs. To achieve compatibility, you might have to standardize your operation with a specific vendor.

- Housing

Your library must be prepared to store, shelve, and move as well as run the equipment. That is, carts are needed to move equipment from storage areas. Sufficient electricity must be available, outlets must be conveniently located, rooms may need to be darkened, and noise may need to be contained.

Processing Equipment

To process equipment when it is delivered, you need to do the following:

- Confirm that appropriate equipment was shipped as ordered.

Determine that all components of a system were shipped as ordered. All necessary accessories were ordered, and these match or work as parts of the equipment. Once connected, the equipment operates as expected. This process differs from a check of print or audiovisual materials received, because, if one item of a shipment of books is missing, the remainder can be used. When components of an equipment system are missing, it is unlikely that the system will operate well or provide all the functions you expected to be able to use.

- Assign and permanently affix an identification number to each item.

An identification number records each piece of equipment as a unique item. The number is used to help keep a record of repairs. It is also used to identify equipment if it is stolen and then located.

- Establish a record card for repairs.

A record card lists date of purchase, vendor, accessories (if applicable), replacement numbers for parts such as bulbs for projecting equipment, and other information, including any warranty that may be in effect. It may list whom to call for repairs, if not your usual repair source. This record will also help with inventory.

Keeping Up with Technology

One of your most difficult tasks may be to keep up with new and ever-changing technologies. As you attend conferences and workshops, you will see new editions of old technologies that require additional or updated software or new pieces to expand an old system. All of these cost money, and you need to budget for these updates. As you begin to save, you must decide how long you can ignore updating your system.

As you consider the continuing barrage of new technologies that will be necessary to keep the information in your library current, you consult with others on the advisability of adding a new technology. A consultant also suggests when to update an old system. This advisor helps you understand when you discard the entire system to select a newer one. Whatever your choice, you must keep your administrators aware of new technologies as they emerge, how much they cost, and the benefits they offer to your users.

DESELECTION OF EQUIPMENT

Discarding equipment seems more difficult than discarding other items, because equipment is more costly to purchase. However, equipment that is out-of-date, whose repair is more expensive than purchasing a new item, and that is likely to malfunction at any time, should be discarded. Maintaining the equipment log shows how often each machine is repaired and when it is costing more to repair than to replace.

POLICY FOR GIFTS

In relation to gifts, the old adage should be reworded, "Always look a gift book in the mouth." Often gifts are inappropriate for the collection, for the following reasons:

- They do not meet the selection criteria outlined in your selection policy, especially relevance to the collection or age of the materials.

- They may be in such poor condition that they are not worth placing in the library collection.

- They may be items that require special handling that you are unable to provide, such as valuable first editions from someone's home library that you could not protect from theft.

Potential gift givers to public libraries and schools may have political, religious, or other beliefs that they would like to espouse. Your collection must address all sides of political issues and represent all religions of the world; however, the gift being offered may be unsubstantiated or biased or the belief may be very esoteric, rather than meeting selection criteria.

COOPERATIVE PURCHASE

Membership in networks has provided opportunities for librarians to join in consortia with cooperative purchase plans. Areas of interest to all are divided among member libraries, and each librarian buys in depth in one or more designated areas, rather than all purchasing a few items in each area. Through interlibrary loan, all items in all libraries are available to all users. If you are involved in any cooperative purchase ventures, you will be responsible for in-depth purchases in certain areas. You must learn when you are to collect materials in these areas, how you notify members of the items purchased, and the mechanisms for handling requests to and from other librarians.

INTELLECTUAL FREEDOM

The concept of intellectual freedom is guaranteed by the First Amendment to the U.S. Constitution. Patrons of libraries have the right to information, and this right should not be limited through librarian censorship of materials. Further, librarians serving patrons in public and school libraries have a responsibility to see that other persons or groups do not cause materials to be removed from library shelves.

Intellectual freedom issues vary from library to library. The American Library Association has an Office for Intellectual Freedom charged with "implementing ALA policies concerning the concept of intellectual freedom as embodied in the Library Bill of Rights, the Association's basic policy on free access to libraries and library materials." [1] This Library Bill of Rights affirms that all libraries are forums for information and ideas, and that the following basic policies should guide their services:

1. Books and other library resources should be provided for the interest, information, and enlightenment of all people of the community the library serves. Materials should not be excluded because of the origin, background, or views of those contributing to their creation.

2. Libraries should provide materials and information presenting all points of view in current and historical issues. Materials should not be proscribed or removed because of partisan or doctrinal disapproval.

3. Libraries should challenge censorship in the fulfillment of their responsibility to provide information and enlightenment.

4. Libraries should cooperate with all persons and groups concerned with resisting abridgment of free expression and free access to ideas.

5. A person's right to use a library should not be denied or abridged because of origin, age, background, or views.

6. Libraries that make exhibit spaces and meeting rooms available to the public they serve should make such facilities available on an equitable basis, regardless of the beliefs or affiliations of individuals or groups requesting their use.

Your type of library will dictate the types of intellectual issues that may be raised. If you are in a school or public library, you are more likely to have requests from parents or others to reconsider materials than if you are in a corporation library. The Library Bill of Rights is your guide in resisting suggestions for inclusion or exclusion of materials. If you have questions or are threatened with a censorship issue, please do not hesitate to contact the association's Office for Intellectual Freedom at their headquarters in Chicago for their assistance.

BUDGET

Library collections grow when funds are available to purchase the needed materials. Because you may have little control over budget for staff or facilities, budget is discussed in this chapter only in relation to additions to the collection.

Funds for the purchase of materials come from a variety of sources. In a school library, the school district budget is passed by the school board. The superintendent allocates building funds through the principal to you. Funds are often distributed on a per-pupil basis. That is, an amount is given for each student. This amount will be multiplied by the number of students, and that is the school library budget. In other situations, you might need to estimate the amount you will need for the entire year and justify each item. With a per-pupil budget, it may be possible to request additional funds if you can justify the need.

Public librarians usually receive their funding from a city council or a library board that redistributes revenues from taxes, endowments, and donations, among others. The public library may have fund-raising activities to increase the budget.

The corporate library is funded by the corporation and corporate library staff may charge back services to their users. Church libraries usually are funded from the budget of their church. Societies or groups within the church may contribute funds for materials.

Whatever the source of funds, you need to become familiar with the method of budgeting and the bookkeeping needed to record how funds are spent. That is, the budget may be a line item or another method.

DECISION THREE: *To prepare the library budget.*

When you prepare the budget depends on how you receive funding. If you must make a case for budget allocations, you decide what you need and what it will cost. When you are given an amount automatically, as in per-pupil allocation, you need only plan how to spend these resources.

Once you have determined the amount of money you will have at your disposal, you will begin to outline proposed expenditures. You will need to know the accounting system your agency uses, so you can divide funds into appropriate categories if this has not already been done.

ACTION ONE: *Learn the budget system.*

Your administrator may have notified you of your budget amount, but you still need to visit the comptroller, accountant, or other fiscal officer and find out the type of budget and methods used to initiate orders, receive shipments, and pay bills. This person can explain regulations for purchases, such as legal requirements for putting orders out for bid.

ACTION TWO: Place proposed expenditures in proper categories.

If you have not received your budget already divided, you will place proposed expenditures into appropriate categories. That is, staff salaries will go under the staff account number; supplies will be placed into another account; materials and equipment in their account; maintenance into that account; telephone and other communication expenses in yet another account; and so on throughout your proposed expenditures.

ACTION THREE: Match proposed expenditures to available resources.

This is the part of budget management that becomes troublesome. Few agencies ever receive as much funding as they would like, and priorities are established. Much discussion has been presented in chapter 7 that establish priorities for purchase of materials and equipment, but similar priorities are set for other items. When travel funds are inadequate, it is necessary to determine who travels to what events. Formulas or other criteria are developed for awarding travel funds.

Justifying Expenditures

When insufficient funds are allocated, you need to justify receiving additional funds from those who distribute funds. Such a case must be made in relationship to the established needs and the probable outcome if more funds are not received. An example of this can be shown with the rising costs of periodical subscriptions. Let's say that the previous year, subscriptions averaged $40 per journal, and you subscribed to 100 journals at $4,000. If your periodicals budget remains at $4,000, yet the average price of subscriptions is now $80 per journal, you will have to cut your subscriptions to only 50. Who will be hurt by this cut? What information will not be available to your users? Although this is a simplistic example, it is an introduction of one method to justify additional funds.

If there is little possibility of increasing the budget from internal sources, external sources may be sought. The next section implies raising funds from external sources; however, the process used externally is equally effective in stating the case for continued funding or new funding from internal sources. Administrators prefer to know that funds allocated will be carefully spent to meet stated needs and fulfill stated objectives.

Raising Funds

When fiscal climates are difficult for local funding, managers are often encouraged to seek outside funding. To do this, you must

- have a good idea at the beginning, usually an original concept;
- find a funding source; and
- write and submit a proposal.

A proposal is made up of a needs statement, goals and objectives, activities, evaluation, dissemination, staff, facilities, time line, and budget. These will be further described in terms of action statements.

DECISION FOUR: *To seek outside resources.*

The following example is described in the context of the need for technology literacy in a library.

ACTION ONE: *To identify needs.*

Identifying needs is a process done in cooperation with other individuals. These may be other members of the library staff; staff and users; administration, staff, and users; staff, users, and recipients of a special service; or any combination of other groups. A needs assessment is more powerful if the needs have been identified by a group rather than a single individual, and most powerful if the recipients of a service proposed are included in the team conducting the needs assessment. A needs statement might say

> The library advisory group made up of A, B, C, D, E, and F expressed their observation that few users were aware of or able to operate Technology X. Yet the research shows that using Technology X has increased productivity in 15 locations. An informal survey of library users confirmed that they wanted Technology X and believed it could increase their efficiency. The survey also determined that only 2 percent of the users were able to operate Technology X, that only 30 percent of users were familiar with or regularly used any information technology beyond the microfiche reader, and that 70 percent would like to learn.

ACTION TWO: *To select probable sources of funding.*

If you borrow someone else's proposal to use as a guideline, that proposal might not meet the guidelines you should follow. Indeed, the example here is only a sample. You must write each proposal to meet the specific request criteria of the funding agency. One suggestion for proposal writing is to target the proposal to the priorities of the funding agency. Therefore, it seems advisable to try to locate a source of funding before beginning to write your proposal.

Most outside funding agencies prefer to fund new ideas rather than make up deficit funding in an agency. Outside funders are not interested that your essentials are severely curtailed. In fact, agencies prefer to fund librarians whose budgets appear to be stable and who will be able to continue any funded program after outside funding has ceased.

Several mechanisms are available for locating funding agencies. This process deserves more than a cursory review, and you are directed to the sources in the annotated bibliography for more details on this.

ACTION THREE: Write goals and objectives.

Not all funding agencies request a goals statement, because a goals statement is broad and overarching and not measurable. An example of such a broad statement might be "to prepare lifelong users of a specific technology." Such a broad statement would be extremely difficult to assess, because you would need to follow each patron who was taught to use this technology.

An objective statement is measurable, and when such a statement is well written, evaluation plans are much easier to write. An objective statement might be "85 percent of users of YY library will become proficient (test of proficiency stated) in the use of Technology X within one year." This statement describes who, how many, what they will do, and within what time frame. This provides a sound basis for the evaluation plan.

ACTION FOUR: State activities.

Activities are written as the means to meet the objectives. For our sample objective, three activities would be

- Introduce users to Technology X in # weekly sessions

- Provide users with Technology X for practice at their workplace

- Hold follow-up sessions to clarify any problems using Technology X

ACTION FIVE: List resources needed.

Resources needed to carry out each activity are listed, with cost for each stated. To carry out our activities, we would need Technology X located where weekly sessions would be held. Either Technology X would be moved from the training location to users' workplaces, or additional systems of Technology X would be acquired to allow users to practice. The follow-up sessions might include question and answer sessions, telephone calls, or additional instruction at the site of the weekly sessions. One cost that is sometimes overlooked is the cost of time of participants. It is a mistake to assume because participants are on salary that there is no cost to their attendance.

In our example, Technology X is available in whatever quantity is needed. Some costs would be associated with hiring trainers, any auxiliary equipment or materials, and the time (salary) of the users while they are in training. Persons participating either as trainer or as learner, when away from their regular assignment, cost someone for their time.

ACTION SIX: Plan evaluation procedures.

Each activity is tested to see the degree to which it is meeting the stated objective. For our sample program, one would only need show that users who had been trained are using Technology X. Time saved and increased productivity, as well as better service, can be shown. If 85 percent of users are proficient within one year, the project would be deemed successful, at least by the standards set in preparing the proposal.

ACTION SEVEN: Explain dissemination.

When projects are funded, most funders wish to have acknowledgment of their participation when the activities are under way. Information concerning favorable outcomes adds prestige to the funding agency, for it shows their good judgment in funding the request. Stating how you plan to tell the appropriate audience about the project, its outcomes, and its contributions are an essential part of your proposal. Dissemination may be in the company newsletter, the local newspaper, through your presentations to service organizations, or in any number of ways.

ACTION EIGHT: Identify staff needed.

Staff needs may be met with your current staff. If so, calculate their time away from their regular jobs as part of the cost of the project. You may wish to donate this time as an in-kind contribution to the project. If you must hire outside trainers, you should write careful job descriptions, state the compensation for their participation, and add this cost to the project.

ACTION NINE: Secure facilities.

Facilities may be available in your library or in a part of your agency, or you may be required to secure facilities elsewhere. If there is a cost to use facilities, this is built into the project budget. If you use your own facilities, you may wish to add the cost of custodial help (if the training goes on after regular work hours) and some reimbursement for the facility. Or you may choose to donate this cost as an in-kind contribution.

ACTION TEN: Create a time line for the project.

Preparing this time line is predicting the future of your project. You need to make a realistic estimate of how long each activity will take. Time is allocated for initial planning of the activities and for each activity as it is put into practice. If you were training users on Technology X, you would include the time given for the weekly sessions. Additional time might be required for a follow-up evaluation three months after the training ends, to see if users were still making good use of Technology X.

ACTION ELEVEN: Prepare budget required.

The budget is tied to the cost of the resources. Staff is one of the costs, and that would be either salary of your own staff or cost of the trainers. Purchase of Technology X in whatever amount is required. Any additional costs involved include telephone, travel and per diem of the trainer, supplies, and other items associated with the project.

This chapter has dealt with adding to your collection, and taking away when weeding, as well as developing a budget. The chapter that follows helps you evaluate what you are doing.

NOTE

1. *ALA Handbook of Organization*. Annual. Chicago: American Library Association.

GLOSSARY

Cataloging-in-publication (CIP). Created by the Library of Congress, CIP is found on the back of the title page and contains part of the information used to create the catalog entry.

Chapter 8

EVALUATING
WHAT YOU DO

Evaluation, in the most basic sense, is counting various program components. This provides instant access to statistics when they are needed such as, "How many books do you have in your library?" and "How many users come into your library in a week?" It gives you evidence of what you are accomplishing. If you have compiled 25 bibliographies this month or provided materials from 57 interlibrary loan requests, you have concrete information about how you are spending your time. This type of information is simple to gather. More difficult is information that has a quality factor.

At some time, someone is going to ask you, "Why?" or "How well?" And if they do not, you will still want to know for yourself how a service is used, how well an activity is being implemented, what programs are most successful, or what you should be but are not doing. This is the process of evaluation.

You need not fear this process. Evaluation shows you those things that you are doing well and those things you should plan to do differently because they are not as successful as you would like them to be. It will also point out those things you should stop doing because no one wants the program or service.

Evaluation schemes exist for everything from analyzing the progress of students in their school programs to determining which is the winning cake at the state fair, and libraries have their fair share. Additional articles and books on evaluation are cited in the annotated bibliography. The purpose of this chapter is to show you some simple techniques for counting and analyzing activities that go on in your library. This will be done with action research methodology that will help you describe "Why?" and "How well?" Both of these questions can sometimes be decided in measuring against someone else's assessment of levels, someone else's yardsticks. Yardsticks or measuring sticks can be found in

- standards and guidelines,

- measuring instruments from articles and books, and

- previous evaluations.

MEASURING AGAINST
STANDARDS AND GUIDELINES

Standards and guidelines are applicable depending on who initiates or imposes them. Standards and guidelines are developed by different organizations for different purposes. The attention you pay to how well you match standards will depend on the power of the agency developing standards to demand that they be met. In some instances, they may be law, and you have a legal responsibility to see that they are met. In other situations, they become goals to achieve. In still others, they may seem to be impossible dreams, and any attempt to reach the standard may seem unimportant.

Standards and guidelines are available from

- state and local funding agencies,

- national and state associations, and

- accrediting agencies.

Standards

Standards are defined in this work as laws governing an operation. Standards are developed by governmental units in an effort to insure equal treatment to all constituencies. Because they are mandated, standards with quantity figures are seldom written in quantities that make it difficult to comply, lest the mandating agency be required to provide sufficient funding to meet the requirement. That is, if the standard for number of items needed for your base library collection is dictated at the state level, it may not be difficult for you to achieve this number because you and your governing board might reasonably expect the state to help you financially to meet their requirement. When a governing body writes standards so low that almost all libraries meet the minimum, you may be penalized when your library exceeds the minimum. That is, your agency may suggest cutting your funds because you meet the state standards.

State agencies may fund libraries only when they have reached an established minimum level. That is, if you are in a group forming a public library in a small community, you may be expected to get enough books, space, and personnel for your library to achieve that minimum level before your library can become part of the government's funding process. Again, this may appear to be more helpful than it is. Libraries that accept donations to make up an inadequate collection and hire all part-time clerical rather than one professional staff in order to meet a minimum standard of personnel with minimum funding may not be serving their patrons well enough to remain viable.

State and local funding agencies with standards are law, and they must be upheld. You should become familiar with any standards and keep your administrators informed of your status in achieving the level required. A simple example of this would be a mandated number of items for your collection, with the number currently in your collection matched to this figure. If your library will only be granted funds from a governmental agency when you have at least 10 books for each user and you have 10,000 users, your library collection should number 100,000. Your local administration may forbid your deselecting items if it means your collection size could drop below the prescribed 100,000 items.

Guidelines

Guidelines may be developed by governmental agencies as guides to programs, but most are written by national and state associations or regional accrediting agencies. Because professional associations are made up of librarians who approve guidelines that describe library programs as they believe they should be, it could appear to outsiders that these persons might have a biased point of view. Although drafts of these documents are reviewed by others in the membership and others in related associations and even the community of users, they still remain the product of a small number of persons, and they are not always based in research. If drafters of guidelines state that no library of a certain type can meet the needs of users with less than 40 items per user and you have 10,000 users, you would need 400,000 volumes. In the case of standards, you must have 100,000 in order to receive funding; with guidelines, your association members state that a much larger number is needed if you are to provide adequate service. However, their statement has no legal status, and you may find your administrators are not interested in this guideline.

Some associations are replacing guidelines with evaluation tools. *Output Measures for Public Libraries*,[1] created by the Public Library Association, a division of the American Library Association, is just such a document. *Output Measures* promotes viewing the library in terms of circulation, in-library materials use, library visits, program attendance, and reference transactions as they relate to per capita use. That is, the library is measured by the number of items circulated from the library in relation to the population of the community.

Reference, Title, Subject, and Author Fill Rates are used to judge the effectiveness of those services. Reference Fill Rate reports the number of references located in terms of the number of references requested; titles include the number of authors, subjects, or titles found in the library when they were requested.

As stated earlier, guidelines are suggestions rather than laws, and they may be goals for you to aspire to. Although they have been developed by professional associations of librarians and may appear to be self-serving, they represent the best thinking of those in the field.

Accrediting agencies also review programs and deem them acceptable. Accreditation is a process most often applied to educational institutions, and you might be involved in accreditation if you are in an elementary, middle/junior high, or high school library. Again, you must clarify the program requirements of the accrediting agency and keep your administrators apprised of your program's status to meet these requirements.

You may consider developing your own guidelines through an analysis of what you wish to achieve. These individually adopted requirements may be the only goal that you have, especially if your library has a state or local funding agency demanding minimum levels or you have no accrediting agency to provide guidelines. A sense of how to evaluate your program and establish guidelines for services is presented later in this chapter.

No matter who sets the standards or guidelines that you choose for measuring your program, you must keep careful records of the items to match to goals. This type of measurement shows how you are achieving and what is yet to be done to meet the standards.

USING SOMEONE ELSE'S
MEASURING INSTRUMENT

Evaluation may be outlined by or in an existing document that includes the actual measuring instruction. One important point must be taken into consideration when applying any instrument to your data. It is often difficult to gather the same information, counting the exact items as requested by the instrument. The example often given for this is the number of volumes found in any library. Does one count an encyclopedia set as "one" or as the number of volumes in any set? For an administrator who is trying to meet some magical requirement, the pressure will be on to count each volume as "one" when, in effect, an encyclopedia set or a two-volume dictionary is only one entity. This lack of standardization in the reporting of data makes it difficult to use evaluation instruments requiring a count of items.

Sources of evaluation information, including techniques and forms, are listed in the annotated bibliography. For those working in schools, an excellent source of evaluation techniques may be found in *Taxonomies of the School Library Media Program*.[2] This will direct you to a variety of methods to assess your program, services, and facility. For instance, a technology evaluation form asks for an evaluation from disagree to agree (five points) for the following:

The theoretical contributions of this equipment have been considered.

The results of research have been analyzed before this technology was adopted.

We know what hardware is available on the commercial market.

We have drawn up specifications for purchase to allow competitive bidding.

We have sought reputable dealers to bid on the equipment.

How often can patron requests to use this equipment be filled?

The sophistication of our equipment meets our level of involvement.

Reviewing someone else's evaluation scheme and evaluation instruments helps you understand what that author considered important. If you have a similar need to know, you may be able to use the evaluation process as it is. Or you may be able to use it with minor adjustments. The author of the original evaluation process may report findings in the literature. If the previous instrument evaluates a situation similar to the research you are conducting, you may be able to compare those results with your results.

If you are applying output measures to public library services, it may well be that such statistics are collected in your state, and you may be able to match your results to those. Applying such results must take into consideration that this process tends to unify the types of information gathered.

One simple evaluation project, shown in appendix G, is adapted from an article by an author in the April 1982 issue of the *NASSP Bulletin*. You may wish to further adapt the chart; you might use some but not all of the questions; or you might choose to use the same areas that are assessed. These areas include an analysis of the various formats in the collection (books, filmstrips, CDs), when the library is open to meet demands, what percentage of potential users use the library, among others. Or you might prefer to use the scale (don't know, not as good as, almost as good as, as good as, better than, or much better than). This evaluation instrument has a point system for the scale from a -1 to a 5. Or you might choose a different method for calculating the score for the answers. An evaluation is taken for the principal and for the media specialist, with an average of teacher and student responses.

PREVIOUS EVALUATIONS

Previous evaluations may have been designed by your predecessor, or they may be the results of information demanded by some agency. They provide you with base data to see if you are adding to or subtracting from the resources available to your users. If they have qualitative parts, you may see if you are improving. If your data are required by a state agency such as the state library or department of education, this information may be useful not only to analyze your progress from one year to the next but also to offer you comparative data to match your library to similar libraries in your region or state.

Formal data gathering may have occurred when reports were filed for these other agencies such as state libraries or departments of education. If an accreditation visit has been made, that report will be in your administrator's office if not in yours. Also, you may have some base data that are stored, meaning that they are not immediately identified as evaluations but can be used as such—circulation statistics, equipment repair records, number of new items purchased, among others.

It is not all that difficult to plan your own evaluation process, because it is unlikely that you are expected to develop a rigorous research project with elaborate data gathering and statistical analysis applied to the findings. Rather, your research should be simple, with practical data carefully gathered to give accurate information. The results need only help you decide what you should keep doing, what you should modify, and what you should stop doing.

The best part of planning and executing your own evaluation is that it is yours, and you need not share the results with anyone. That way you can begin to make appropriate improvements before you face a required review.

PLANNING YOUR OWN

Planning your own evaluation allows you to look at specific items in which you are interested. You may adapt any evaluation form to exclude unneeded items, or you may develop your own questions. Researchers will tell you that there are two pitfalls into which you may slip. The first is that you may ask for information that is in the "nice to know" category rather than the "necessary to know." That is, you should not ask for information that you do not need. In the outside world, many researchers ask for age and sex when that information has no real bearing on their research. Such requests may, in fact, lessen your chances of getting the information you want.

The second pitfall is that you should not develop questions that bias the response. This means those in the category of "When did you stop kicking your dog?" If you ask users to indicate the importance they place on various library services and you list only those services that you consider important without giving them an opportunity to add to your list, you are allowing bias to creep into the responses.

Some sample questions you might ask are shown in figure 8.1:

Prioritize services offered by their importance to you, giving 12 to the most important and 1 to the least important.

_____ newspapers, local

_____ newspapers, national

_____ periodicals

_____ CD-ROM databases

_____ reference books such as encyclopedias and almanacs

_____ fiction books for leisure reading

_____ children's story hour

_____ programming for day care centers

_____ programming for senior citizen centers and nursing homes

_____ job information center

_____ other, please specify _____

_____ other, please specify _____

Fig. 8.1. Sample questionnaire for gauging importance of services.

After users have ranked these services, you need only total the scores. The one receiving the highest number will be the most preferred service of those ranking the services.

This is one way to begin to assess your program. The analyses suggested below are other simple suggestions that will take you through one evaluation exercise. It is hoped that you will be encouraged and inspired enough to do a second.

Time on Task

To analyze how long it takes to accomplish any task, keep a log book of what happens through the day. For example, log each reference question and how long it takes to find the answer. You can log telephone calls to see how many you receive each day, recording the purpose of the call and how long it takes you to complete any activity related to the call. You can also log mail received and how long it takes you to answer the mail. It is unlikely that you will be able to hire a time management expert, but you do need to see how much of your time is spent on various tasks in your library.

Staffing Analysis

Suppose your administrator suggests or a user survey indicates a task that should be added to your already crowded day. In chapter 3, tasks and time allocations were shown in relation to the job description. Using this information as an example, your activities, when translated into a daily diary of experience, might look like the following chart: Please note that the times have been rounded off for ease of calculation.

Day One

%	Hours	Project
3	8:00-8:15	Open facility, review daily calendar.
3	8:15-8:30	Start up all machinery, check working order.
3	8:30-8:45	Open mail, read E-mail, respond to correspondence.
3	8:45-9:00	Check status of purchase orders.
12	9:00-10:00	Meet with J—, department head, to discuss periodicals budget and probable purchase for next year.
24	10:00-12:00	Reference desk: Conduct online searches and collect information requested on topics.
	12:00-1:00	Monthly lunch with department heads.
6	1:00-1:30	Schedule remaining periodicals budget appointments with secretaries of department heads. This process due by end of week.
6	1:30-2:00	Print out bibliography and collect information for administrator who is writing a speech.
24	2:00-4:00	Reference desk.
12	4:00-5:00	Shelve items that have been returned.

Day Two

%	Hours	Project
3	8:00-8:15	Open facility, review daily calendar.
3	8:15-8:30	Start up all machinery, checking working order.
3	8:30-8:45	Open mail, read E-mail, respond to correspondence.
9	8:45-9:30	Continue shelving items on shelves.
12	9:30-10:30	Meet with K—, department head, to discuss periodicals budget and probable purchases for next year.
24	10:30-12:30	Reference desk: Conduct online searches and collect information requested on topics.
	12:30-1:00	Lunch.
12	1:00-2:00	Meet with M—, department head, to discuss periodicals budget and probable purchases for next year.
24	2:00-4:00	Reference desk.
12	4:00-5:00	Shelve items that have been returned.

If you were to place the above into categories and average your time, you would find that your days were spent as shown in figure 8.2:

A = Administrative (contacts out of library)
C = Clerical
R = Reference
M = Management in library

Day 1	Day 2
3 (M)	3 (M)
3 (M)	3 (M)
3 (M)	3 (M)
3 (M)	9 (C)
12 (A)	12 (A)
24 (R)	24 (R)
6 (C)	12 (A)
6 (C)	24 (R)
24 (R)	12 (C)
12 (C)	

Average Percentage of Time Spent at Tasks

Day One percent + Day Two percent = $\dfrac{\text{Total percent}}{2}$ = Average percent

Management: 12 + 9 = 21 or 11%

Clerical:24 + 21 = 45 or 22%

Reference: 48 + 48 = 96 or 48%

Administrative: 12 + 24 = 36 or 18%

Fig. 8.2.

Figure 8.2 demonstrates that, on the average, you spend more time on clerical tasks (22%) than on management. Further, almost half of your time is assigned to the reference desk. If outreach is a major factor, then the 18 percent average is not sufficient, and you should seek ways to reduce clerical time so that you can spend your time on more appropriate or desirable activities.

This is a simplistic example of calculating time allocations. However, it is the author's belief that the amount of time allocated to evaluation should not exceed the time devoted to accomplishing the tasks you are evaluating. Further, you may have to schedule the time to evaluate, and that may be based on several factors.

User Satisfaction

DECISION ONE: When to evaluate.

Evaluation should occur when the need arises. Sometimes this need is determined not by you but by administrators or funding agencies. That is, your state status report may be due in the state library on July 1.

If you are initiating an evaluation study yourself, you will obviously begin to evaluate as information is needed, for example, when you begin to plan for the next year's budget, for specific selections and additions to your collection, or when you must add or subtract hours from staff. You should evaluate your services at least once every two years, to confirm that you are meeting user needs.

DECISION TWO: What to evaluate.

Knowing what users value about your services is of primary importance in planning for your library. You can do this in a variety of ways, such as asking individual users as they come in to return or take out materials. If this is your form of evaluation, you must keep a log book handy to write in their comments, or it is likely that you will forget them before you have time to make a record.

You can also ask users to rank services, ranging from what they appreciate most to what they use the least. This will give you an indication of who is using what services, and you can match this to any records you may have substantiating use. That is, if users say they are using one area of the collection most of all, but you are not aware of this use, that is, circulation records do not show this use, you may need to ask if they are using the materials in the library rather than checking them out, and what has precipitated the use. You can then ask if you have sufficient materials to meet their needs. Figure 8.3 shows an example of a user survey form.

Today I was looking for materials
(check all that apply)

_____ nonfiction

_____ fiction

_____ reference

Materials were sufficient to meet my needs?

not at all   somewhat   mostly   very much

I would like more information on:

Fig. 8.3. User survey form.

More elaborate surveys can be conducted, using short to much longer questionnaires. The length of the questionnaire may affect the number of responses you get, for if it is too long, patrons may not take the time to answer. You must test any questionnaire to confirm that what you have asked is what the reader understands, and the answers you get are in response to what you thought you asked. For instance, a user might respond "never" to the question, "How often do you ask for database searches?" In fact the person is a heavy database user who uses your CD-ROM collection rather than an online search. If someone other than yourself administers the survey, you must take care not only that they understand the question, but that their answers will be reported so that you understand the response.

Facilities evaluations begin with your review of what your library really looks like when you walk in the door. Too many persons accept the way a library looks rather than try to correct things that could be modified with little or no expenditure of funds. Would posters on walls, especially if they are from book publishers, be a low-cost means to brighten the reading room? Would plants add to the general ambiance? Would reducing the clutter be possible?

Do your users notice the ambiance? Again, you can make one or two changes and see if these are noticed. If they are, you may wish to ask what other changes could be suggested. Often your users may have good suggestions that will help you improve the look of the facility.

Services and their evaluation, in terms of which to offer and which to delete, have been mentioned in chapter 6. However, you may wish to survey your users to gauge their satisfaction with levels of service. Would they prefer that you provide them with materials, or do they prefer to look for themselves? If you are to do in-depth searches for them, what other service should or could be cut? This form of evaluation helps take the total responsibility for removal of a less-used service from you solely and makes it a joint decision.

Collection Development

Information gathered from users related to your collection may be of great help or it may not be useful at all. Nevertheless, a form that measures usefulness should be completed by you or your user or both when materials are returned. This enables you to rethink what you provide for users in their subsequent searches or for others searching for information on that topic. Certainly if materials are dated, you need to know, so that you can discard and replace. If more materials are needed, you will have the evidence that they should be purchased. When the needs are more than the available budget, this evidence will help you make a case for additional funding.

If you have nonusers, it may be that what they need is not found in the library. Therefore, you may need to survey your nonusers to ask them why they do not use your library collection.

Evaluating a Proposed Service

If your users agree with you or suggest independently that a new service is needed, it may be that this new service will place an unusual burden on the budget. For some, the solution would be to charge a fee for service. Your users may want you to prepare full text reproductions of important journal articles for them. An evaluation form for this proposed service might look like figure 8.4:

We are considering full text reproduction of articles in your area of interest. Because we do not have sufficient funding to cover the cost of copying, we are asking you to respond to the following:		
	Yes	No
1. Having full text reproduction is an important service.	_____	_____
2. I would be willing to pay for any copies of documents.	_____	_____
3. My department should be willing to pay for copies for me.	_____	_____
4. A suitable fee would be $.10 per page.	_____	_____
5. A suitable fee would be $.20 per page.	_____	_____
6. Any cost up to $.50 per page would be suitable.	_____	_____

Fig. 8.4. A user evaluation form for a proposed service.

If your users are willing to pay for the service, you may choose to begin the service under a fee structure. If they are not, you then ask them to rank services to see what must go and what can stay.

Ranking Services

As mentioned earlier, present services can be ranked based on user satisfaction. Services may also be ranked to see if suggested new services receive a higher priority than existing services. In the case of full text reproduction, you might ask users to rank services, using the questionnaire in figure 8.5, on page 142.

Many of our users have asked us to consider offering full text reproduction of important articles. Would you please rank the following services from 1 to 5 (1 being preferred service and 5 less preferred) so that we can determine preferred services?

_____ full text reproduction

_____ full text reproduction only up to 20 articles per year

_____ current contents posting of periodicals in collection

_____ cut periodicals budget by 10%

_____ wait and purchase periodicals on microfilm

Fig. 8.5. Questionnaire for user ranking of services.

Or you may wish to ask users to assign a percentage of budget to each of the materials and services listed in figure 8.6.

_____ books

_____ periodicals

_____ periodicals on microfilm

_____ research reports

_____ government documents

_____ dissertations

_____ full text reproduction

_____ online database searching

_____ clipping services

Fig. 8.6.

Reporting Your Findings

Once you have collected evaluative data, you must decide how to analyze the data. You may want to total rankings to find the highest number and make that service the winner. Other suggestions for collecting and analyzing data can be found in the bibliography.

Should you choose to report your findings, the results, whether given orally or written, must be prepared in simple language that can be easily understood by the listener or reader. Well-designed charts and graphs can further understanding.

The evaluation methods you choose, how often you evaluate, and who receives the data are all decisions for you to make in developing your own instrument. Whether you must do an evaluation for an outside agency or because you want to know something about user satisfaction with your services, the important thing is to be prepared to evaluate your program and services. If you do not evaluate, you will not know what you are doing well. Even if you sense that you are meeting the needs of your users, you will have no real proof if you are not asking questions and getting answers.

NOTES

1. Douglas Zweizig and Eleanor Jo Rodger, *Output Measures for Public Libraries: A Manual of Standardized Procedures*. Chicago: American Library Association, 1982.

2. David V. Loertscher, *Taxonomies of the School Library Media Program*. Englewood, Colo.: Libraries Unlimited, 1988. pp. 116-17.

Chapter 9

CREATING A LIBRARY WHERE NONE EXISTS

If you have never worked in a library or taken any library science courses in a college or university, you should hope to inherit an existing library. Your library is there. You need only review the facility, match services to user needs, and check the collection for usefulness, among other tasks. Although this is no small assignment, it does not present the hazards and pitfalls of beginning a library from scratch.

To prepare a facility where none exists, you must begin at the very beginning of the design and implementation steps for all areas and all activities. By any definition you are building a library. It may be that building translates into "remodeling an existing space," but you will be planning as if you were building from the basement to the roof or from the floor to the ceiling (if you are a part of a larger building). You will need to work closely with those who will be funding the center to discuss the budget for this endeavor.

From choosing location through the selection and placement of your newly acquired collection and furniture to opening the doors for your first patrons, you must work carefully. You will be preparing a library for users who will need to be shown how to use the information, where things are located, and how to use your services. Most of these decisions will require professional expertise. Mistakes made at the beginning may become difficult to correct later. When managing your library carries the responsibility of choosing a location, selecting the furniture and equipment, buying the initial collection, and arranging the furniture, you should definitely ▣**Ask a Librarian** or request funding to pay a consultant.

A consultant will help you choose the best among the various alternatives. This only confirms that two heads are better than one.

WHERE TO LOCATE

Your library should be located as close to your clientele as possible. For the public library, this means in a population center; on a site that is attractive; in a building that is inviting, large enough for the present and for some future expansion; and near or in major gathering points such as shopping centers, main business areas, or other areas where there is a great deal of traffic. Unfortunately, you may be offered an empty room in city hall next to the jail, or an abandoned school, or some board member's unoccupied store.

Three major problems often occur in using an existing building. Many buildings lack handicapped access. Preparing ramps and installing elevators for access are often expensive. The building must be capable of supporting the weight of materials and shelving to be housed there. Few persons can imagine the actual weight of books on shelves. Also, patrons need to be able to park easily and close to the library, and there should be sufficient parking spaces.

Buildings that are not built to be libraries are real challenges to the creativity of the person planning the remodeling, and sometimes it is virtually impossible to make it work. For instance, ceilings may be very high, making the building difficult to heat; acoustics may be poor; and the sense of being in a warehouse or barn will not attract patrons. In using an available site, you may not be close to patrons, and you may be in a less desirable neighborhood. However, many things that, at first sight, appear to be insurmountable, at second or third review turn out to be a challenge that can be met.

In a school, your location should be in the center of the classroom area. Again, you may be offered a large coat closet near the cafeteria; the walls around a cafeteria; the back of the gymnasium; the basement area in front of the doors to the office, bathrooms, and lunch room; or a Quonset hut off the parking lot, most recently used by the shop teachers. All of these have been converted into libraries in the experience of this author. For any size school, you will need an area at least as large as a regular classroom. It is often simple to remove the wall between two adjacent classrooms to make a usable library. With creativity in the arrangement of the library, the room can accommodate the four walls that you will inherit.

Special libraries should be located near where the heavy users are working. When users are close to the information they need, getting to the library provides a brief break in the otherwise busy day.

And so, you choose the location most central to your users and work with what you are assigned. The point is that you make any location as attractive as possible so that users are drawn to the facility no matter where it is located.

Once the location has been chosen, you must plan the arrangement of the furniture and select the furniture, equipment, and collection. Finally, you will locate the furnishings in the room or rooms as you have planned. It is time to 📖**Ask a Librarian.**

At this point, you may wish to visit other libraries to see how they have been arranged, what equipment and furniture are in use there, and how these libraries look as you walk through the door. The librarian will be able to tell you what works well and what changes could be made for a more efficient operation. Getting helpful hints concerning equipment, its uses and repair, manufacturers who provide high-quality products, and so on will make your visit well worth the time. Then you will be better prepared to consider placement of chairs and tables, what furniture you will need for your patrons to make the best use of your facility, and to choose your furniture.

PLANNING THE ARRANGEMENT OF FURNISHINGS

Arranging a space for any purpose depends upon the size of the space, doors and windows that must be kept unobstructed, and any other physical features that affect the furnishings you choose. Traditionally, tall shelving is placed against the walls. However, you may need to select shelving to arrange open spaces into special areas of the library. You will want to map how each piece of furniture fits into the available spaces. For this you can use a scale grid, remembering that spaces are needed between tables, chairs, shelves, and desks for patrons to walk and for you to move book trucks and equipment carts to and from shelving. If you are meeting specifications for handicapped patrons, aisles must accommodate a wheelchair.

SELECTING FURNITURE

Selecting furniture will depend on the amount of space you have, the number of users you must accommodate, the amount of materials that you must house, the equipment you must store, and the types of activities that will go on in your library. If most of your materials are in microform, you need only cabinets to store microfilm and microfiche, readers and printers, and any automation that is available to provide access to your collection. Integrating all formats requires adjustable shelves.

Furniture must accommodate most of your users. In elementary schools and children's departments in public libraries, chairs and tables are smaller. Special furniture such as a sloping-top picture-book table is needed. Small public libraries need more comfortable seating for patrons to read newspapers and magazines.

Furniture should match. That is, tables and shelving should be purchased from the same supply house. In schools and public libraries, this is based on a bidding process to get you the best price possible. In some cases, furniture such as shelving is constructed, with chairs and tables purchased from another source. Libraries with matching furniture and shelving almost always look nicer than those with furnishings ordered from several sources. You will not want your library to look as if it were built from visits to flea markets and garage sales. Sometimes when libraries look like they were furnished from garage sales, they are treated that way.

ARRANGING THE FURNITURE

Because you will have drawn a grid and placed furniture throughout the space before actually ordering tables, chairs, shelves, chargeout desk, filing cabinets, computer tables, magazine storage and lounge furniture, once the library facility is painted and carpeted, you need only place the furniture where you planned for it to be. If it does not fit, you can do some rearranging immediately. If your planning was not as good as you might have liked, rearrange before the facility opens.

After you have been in your facility for some time, reassess how everything is working. You may need to rearrange , using the information in chapter 2 about traffic patterns and quiet and noisy areas.

SELECTING EQUIPMENT

Equipment for use in library management, such as online public access catalogs or automated circulation systems, is selected to match the technology recording the holdings of neighboring libraries whenever possible. In this way, it will be easier to share resources among librarians.

Refer to chapter 7, on collection development, concerning the need to keep records of warranties, repairs, and other information that would be helpful in choosing when and what to replace when equipment stops performing well.

SELECTING THE COLLECTION

Selecting a basic collection for any library is difficult and time-consuming. It is difficult because you do not want to make any mistakes. You will need to ask your users what types of materials they want to use.

In some schools, materials may be located in classroom collections. If this is true, the materials should be centrally processed, so central records are kept. Each year the room collection should be reviewed to see that materials are suitable for the collection at grade level, relevant, recent, and in good enough condition that they will stand more circulation. When classroom collections are joined to form a central library, they must meet the criteria assigned to all new additions, even though they are currently available for addition to your collection. You do not wish to be so hungry for materials that you will accept the findings from attics or basements or the discards from the church bazaar that have found their way into the classroom collection.

Chapter 10

INCREASING YOUR SKILLS AS A LIBRARIAN

When you find that you need more information on how to manage your library, a variety of resources are available. Throughout this book, it was indicated when it would be appropriate to seek out and 📖**Ask a Librarian**.

This, however, offers short-term solutions to what may become long-term problems.

Although librarians in nearby libraries are willing to answer questions, they may not be immediately available when your problem arises. Also, the problem may require more help than can be given in a brief telephone call. Further, it may be difficult for you to explain the problem correctly, so that it is understood by the listener. It is similar to understanding patrons with reference questions. If you do not understand their questions, you are more likely to give them unneeded information or incorrect answers. It is far better for you to take as many opportunities as possible to gain additional education and experience.

For some persons expected to run a library, continuing education is essential, if not mandatory, particularly as new information resources are created and technology changes. Necessary educational experiences may be part of the contractual agreement, and remuneration is made for your efforts in one of several ways: release time to attend, payment of fees including travel to a distant location, and increased salary when the experiences have been completed.

There are several ways to expand your knowledge: formal courses for college or university credits, continuing education classes offered by institutions of higher education, workshops, conferences, hiring consultants, and reading. These will be discussed in relation to achieving a license to practice, formal education to earn a degree, and less formal experiences at workshops or conferences.

LICENSE TO PRACTICE

Persons working in special libraries or managing libraries for their churches will have few regulations placed on them. However, this is not true for public or school librarians. Depending on the size or type of library, one receives a "license" to practice in a public library based on the requirements of those responsible for assuring that information is provided by persons who have the skills to provide it. For public libraries, the size of the population served is usually the yardstick, and qualifications may range from no educational requirements at all to specific levels of education or even specific courses. That is, larger libraries may require that all librarians hold a master's in library science from a college or university whose library science program is accredited by the American Library Association (ALA). A list of these programs is available from the Accreditation Officer, American Library Association, 50 E. Huron Street, Chicago, IL 60611.

Requirements vary by state, and you should be aware of any requirements in your state for the type of library you are managing. In some states the requirement is a degree from an ALA-accredited program. In others, you may take course work at any state institution. This is usually the case for school librarians who may complete requirements for their teacher's certificate in a school of education.

In many locations, it is possible to complete your course work in a distance education program. In these, courses are offered where students are living, so they need not move to a college and live in housing there to complete requirements.

Check with the state library or the state department of education to confirm that a program you would like to enroll in will give you the degree or certificate to work in the library of your choice. If there is a problem with that institution, you would be wise to choose another. Other librarians may offer helpful suggestions of schools that provide courses.

Another type of employee for libraries is the library technician. Programs in community colleges train people to work in technical positions in libraries when they have completed an associate of arts degree.

Many institutions of higher education provide library science instruction in a variety of departments within schools of education or in schools of library and information science, leading to certification to work as a school librarian. Other colleges and schools offer undergraduate courses, allowing a student to minor in library science at the bachelor's level and prepare to manage a school library. Graduates of these four-year institutions may be teacher certified to work in school libraries in their state. Depending on individual state regulations, this may be the only educational experience required for school librarians.

If you are teaching in a school and already hold certification, you may be able to expand your license or certificate to teach by adding an endorsement as a school librarian through additional course work at the undergraduate level. For those persons who hold a bachelor's degree in a different discipline, some courses may be required in educational philosophy and psychology, teaching methodology, and motivating learners, among others. A telephone call to a nearby college or university with library science courses will start you on your path to full certification. Certification in some states leads to an actual school librarian's license, in others to a media specialist's license, and in still others to a library media specialist's license. It's all in the name.

For those with little or no experience in higher education, formal education toward a bachelor's degree may seem a long effort, but the result is worth the energy and money you will invest.

FORMAL EDUCATION

Degree and certification programs are considered formal education because they follow established procedures, have uniform curriculum guidelines with a number of required course choices, dictate a method of assessment that results in grades and the computation of quality point averages, and result in a legal document, a diploma, or a license.

Schools of education provide courses leading to a master's degree in education with teacher/librarian certification. These programs also offer you an opportunity to earn your license to practice in a school library. Such programs meet state requirements for the state in which the college or university is located, although some programs in schools of education prepare all types of librarians. When programs are offered in some state-supported institutions, graduates and persons earning certification may be hired in all state-supported public and academic libraries, whether or not they have a master's degree from an ALA-accredited program.

Whether attending schools with course work at the undergraduate or graduate level, you want to be sure you are in an approved program. Programs in schools of education are part of the review process of the entire school of education when they are reviewed and accredited by regional accrediting agencies such as Middle States and a national accrediting agency such as the National Council for the Accreditation of Teacher Education (NCATE). These mean that programs meet the guidelines established not only by their state but by these regional and national agencies.

Programs accredited by the ALA's Committee on Accreditation prepare graduates at the master's level to work in academic, public, school, and special libraries. For many librarians, the master's in library science from an ALA-accredited program is the "license" to practice in public and academic libraries. These are often offered in programs that are in schools of a university or in a department within a larger school.

Attending regular classes at colleges and universities may be difficult if these institutions are not located close to you. Registration for classes follows procedures for matriculating at the college, and persons interested in attending must get information concerning the requirements for enrollment from each school. Because courses are for regular credit, the cost of attending will be the cost of tuition.

When you choose to increase your skills through an academic route, you will become more cognizant of the role of the librarian and the functions of the library from a theoretical point. Learning the theory to match your practice is helpful when you need to know why something is done the way it is or why one choice is better than another when you make a management decision about some aspect of your library.

Many of the degree programs have field experiences for their students. With these opportunities, students are given apprentice-type assignments, working alongside an expert for up to six or eight weeks. They learn the nitty-gritty chores of the library, practice helping patrons, expand their knowledge of reference sources and database searching, circulate materials, pull requested collections of materials, develop bibliographies, and so on. You can replicate this type of experience by spending one or two days with a librarian in the same type of library that you are managing.

Many colleges and universities as well as other agencies offer informal programs. These provide excellent opportunities to learn to practice. These continuing education programs are useful for practitioners who wish to keep up-to-date. When schools of education and schools of library and information science offer such experiences, these programs are usually scheduled for shorter periods of time, with alternative schedules such as three days or a week in vacation periods, or over the weekend. Such times are more amenable to the schedules of full-time employees. Sometimes such offerings are for college credit, but more often they are for continuing education units, and the cost is often much less than for courses taken for college credit.

JOINING A PROFESSIONAL ASSOCIATION

Belonging to a professional association is another excellent way to increase your professional skills. You may find professional associations at the local, state, and national levels. Some local associations are affiliates of the larger state or national association. It may be that you must pay membership fees to the national association to participate in the local or state association activities. You will receive the association's newsletter or periodical, be eligible to attend local, regional, state, or national conferences, and let the association help you remain fully informed.

Attendance at meetings of professional associations is an excellent way to meet librarians and information professionals and to hear a variety of speakers who will be offering information that is new and exciting. Most professional associations also have exhibits with the latest publications and the newest technologies. Equipment is available for demonstration, and you can meet and talk with salespersons to learn about their products. A list of professional associations with dues for membership, number of members, and when they hold national conferences is given in appendix C.

LESS FORMAL OPPORTUNITIES

Less formal opportunities include workshops and informal visits. Workshops may be offered by anyone who can attract an audience. Consultants, individuals, professional associations, school districts, public library personnel, social groups, service organizations, and staff members of libraries may all decide that a topic is essential to bring librarians up-to-date on a new technology, a new process, a new idea, a new method. Brochures are created and mailed, and the opportunity is given to participate. These may carry continuing education credit, or they may just be for personal satisfaction.

One informal means is to visit librarians in other libraries when their schedules and yours permit. Even veteran librarians are always interested in how someone in a similar position accomplishes similar tasks. Telephone calls and planned brief visits are the minimum means you can use to increase your skills, but they can also be effective. They probably will not be enough for every situation, but they can help you see many different ways to carry out the management of your library.

Whether you become involved in a professional association or continue to attend workshops, you will be rewarded for your attendance because you will meet others working in similar situations. You will be able to trade horror stories as well as relate your successes. Sharing ideas is an excellent way to expand your horizons.

Hiring a Consultant

At some time you may have to undertake a task that calls for additional expertise for a longer period of time. When that type of problem arises, hiring a consultant to review the situation may be the best or only solution. A consultant can propose alternatives to the troublesome situation and help you determine which solution will fit your needs and your budget. Many varied situations exist that would prompt you to ask for outside help, many types of consultants are available, and the cost for their expertise varies as much as the problems. The author suggests that you 📖**Ask a Librarian** or review the readings in the annotated bibliography, then make your plans.

Reading on Your Own

Many persons have been self-taught. Certainly the basics of library management can be found in the library literature. One of the benefits of more formal education is that you have someone with whom to discuss issues and share in the presentation of new ideas, theories, impact of historical events on present library services, and other points. However, this may not be a possibility for the immediate future. See the annotated bibliography arranged by general area of management, and begin your education.

Information in this book has been collected to offer ideas for procedures, methods, and suggestions for success when you are given the responsibility for a library. Offering your service to others by helping them to choose books to read for pleasure and for information and to find the perfect answers to their questions is truly challenging and worthwhile. It is hoped that this book will help you do it right the first time, thereby expanding your pleasure in running your library.

APPENDIX A
NONUSER SURVEY

LOCATION_____ TIME_____

INTERVIEWER_____ DATE_____

1. Do you know where our library is located? _____ Yes _____ No

   If yes, do you use our library? _____ Yes _____ No

   If no, why don't you use our library?

____ Too far from home.	____I'm afraid I will lose the book.
____ Did not know it was free.	____I find it hard to read.
____ Never have what I want.	____Not open when I can go.
____ I do not have a card.	____Other (please explain)_____
____ I buy all my materials.	_____
____ I do not have time.	____Do not know.

2. Do you use other libraries? _____ Yes _____ No

3. Do you know about our library? _____ Yes _____ No

4. Where do you live? _____North _____South _____East _____West

5. Do you know how to get a library card? _____ Yes _____ No If no,

   Are you interested in getting a library card? _____ Yes _____ No

6. If you went to the library, what would you like to find there?

_____ books	_____ phonorecords	_____ reference help
_____ magazines	_____ videocassettes	_____ copy machine
_____ newspapers	_____ framed prints	_____ Internet access

7. What subject matter would you be most interested in?

_____ philosophy   _____ the arts
_____ religion   _____ literature, poetry, plays, humor
_____ social science   _____ fiction
_____ language, grammar   _____ general information
_____ science, math, astronomy
_____ technology, medical, gardening, cooking

8. When is the most convenient time for you to use the library?

_____Before Noon _____ Before 5:00 P.M. _____ After 5:00 P.M.

9. Age   _____ under 14   _____ 41-50
           _____ 14-20   _____ 51-60
           _____ 21-30   _____ 61-70
           _____ 31-40   _____ over 70

10. Sex _____ female _____ male

APPENDIX B
EXAMPLES OF JOB APPLICATIONS

DP 1
Rev 10/1/91

PITTSBURGH BOARD OF PUBLIC EDUCATION
APPLICATION FOR PROFESSIONAL EMPLOYMENT

PLEASE PRINT OR TYPE.

GENERAL INFORMATION

POSITION APPLIED FOR	DATE AVAILABLE FOR EMPLOYMENT

NAME	SOCIAL SECURITY NUMBER

PRESENT TELEPHONE
( )

TEMPORARY ADDRESS ___ NUMBER AND STREET   CITY   STATE   ZIP CODE

PERMANENT TELEPHONE
( )

PERMANENT ADDRESS ___ NUMBER AND STREET   CITY   STATE   ZIP CODE

Are You a U.S. Citizen?
☐ Yes ☐ No
If NO, give Alien Registration Number

WERE YOU PREVIOUSLY EMPLOYED HERE?   YES ☐   NO ☐   IF YES, WHEN?
POSITION   UNDER WHAT NAME?

Have you ever pleaded guilty to, or been convicted of any violation other than a misdemeanor or summary offense?
☐ Yes ☐ No
If Yes Describe in full

MILITARY SERVICE

BRANCH OF ARMED SERVICE	Active Duty				Rank		Major Duties/Specialty Training
	From		To		Entry	Release	
	Mo.	Yr.	Mo.	Yr.			

RESERVE STATUS					BRANCH		

EDUCATION

G.E.D.:   Yes ☐   No ☐

NAME OF SCHOOL & LOCATION (City and State) (Include all institutions attended)	DATES ATTENDED		YEAR GRAD	DEGREE OBTAINED	COURSE or MAJOR STUDY
	FROM	TO			

CERTIFICATION

CERTIFIED: ☐ Yes ☐ No ☐ APPLYING OR HAVE APPLIED	LIST SUBJECTS YOU ARE CERTIFIED TO TEACH OR SUBJECTS FOR WHICH YOU EXPECT TO RECEIVE CERTIFICATION
IF YES, CHECK THE PENNSYLVANIA CERTIFICATION WHICH APPLIES: ☐ INSTRUCTIONAL I ☐ EDUCATIONAL SPECIALIST I ☐ INSTRUCTIONAL II (PERMANENT) ☐ EDUCATIONAL SPECIALIST II (PERM.)	

List (3) three references who have known you in a professional capacity.
NOTE: New graduates should list individuals who have supervised their student teaching.
Also, if you have a placement folder, please have it sent.

REFERENCES		
NAME	OCCUPATON	
ADDRESS	PHONE ( )	
NAME	OCCUPATION	
ADDRESS	PHONE ( )	
NAME	OCCUPATION	
ADDRESS	PHONE ( )	

STUDENT TEACHING EXPERIENCE

ADDRESS SCHOOL DISTRICT STATE	NO. OF MONTHS	GRADE(S)	SUBJECT	DATES FROM	TO

LIST MOST RECENT FIRST.

TEACHING EMPLOYMENT HISTORY

MONTH AND YEAR	SCHOOL DISTRICT NAME AND ADDRESS	SUBJECT	GRADE
FROM		REASON FOR LEAVING	
TO			
SUPERVISOR	TELEPHONE NUMBER		
MONTH AND YEAR	SCHOOL DISTRICT NAME AND ADDRESS	SUBJECT	GRADE
FROM		REASON FOR LEAVING	
TO			
SUPERVISOR	TELEPHONE NUMBER		
MONTH AND YEAR	SCHOOL DISTRICT NAME AND ADDRESS	SUBJECT	GRADE
FROM		REASON FOR LEAVING	
TO			
SUPERVISOR	TELEPHONE NUMBER		
MONTH AND YEAR	SCHOOL DISTRICT NAME AND ADDRESS	SUBJECT	GRADE
FROM		REASON FOR LEAVING	
TO			
SUPERVISOR	TELEPHONE NUMBER		

Please indicate permission to check references at your present place of employment. ☐ Yes   ☐ No

LIST MOST RECENT FIRST.

NON-TEACHING EMPLOYMENT HISTORY

MONTH AND YEAR	EMPLOYER NAME AND ADDRESS	POSITION	SUPERVISOR
FROM		REASON FOR LEAVING	
TO			
FINAL SALARY	TELEPHONE NUMBER		

MONTH AND YEAR	EMPLOYER NAME AND ADDRESS	POSITION	SUPERVISOR
FROM		REASON FOR LEAVING	
TO			
FINAL SALARY	TELEPHONE NUMBER		

MONTH AND YEAR	EMPLOYER NAME AND ADDRESS	POSITION	SUPERVISOR
FROM		REASON FOR LEAVING	
TO			
FINAL SALARY	TELEPHONE NUMBER		

MONTH AND YEAR	EMPLOYER NAME AND ADDRESS	POSITION	SUPERVISOR
FROM		REASON FOR LEAVING	
TO			
FINAL SALARY	TELEPHONE NUMBER		

Please indicate permission to check references at your present place of employment. ☐ Yes ☐ No

COLLEGE & COMMUNITY ACTIVITIES

ORGANIZATION	FROM	TO

The Pittsburgh Public School District is an equal opportunity education institution and will not discriminate on the basis of age, race, religion, color, national origin, sex, or handicap in its activities, programs, or employment practices in compliance with Title VI and VII of the Civil Rights Act of 1964 as amended, the Age Discrimination and Employment Act, the Pennsylvania Human Relations Act, the Federal Rehabilitation Act, and all subsequent laws and orders that pertain to Equal Employment Opportunity. For information regarding civil rights or grievance procedures, contact: Office of Contract Compliance, Pittsburgh Public Schools, 341 South Bellefield Avenue, Pittsburgh, PA 15213 (412) 622-3610.

I hereby certify that the foregoing information and statements are true, and I understand that misrepresentation or omission of the facts called for herein will be sufficient cause for rejection of the application or for dismissal if such information is discovered subsequent to my employment. I agree to take any job-related tests or medical examinations whenever required by the Pittsburgh Board of Public Education whether prior to or subsequent to employment. I understand that an offer of employment with the Board is contingent upon my satisfactorily passing the pre-employment physical examination required by the Board and receipt of an Act 33 Child Abuse Clearance and/or Act 34 Criminal History Record Information check. I authorize and instruct the Pittsburgh Board of Public Education to investigate any and all statements contained in this application of any person(s) and/or organization(s) who are not a consumer reporting agency.

_____ _____
Applicant's Signature   Date

TO BE FILLED IN BY DIVISION OF PERSONNEL ONLY

ELIGIBILITY LIST INFORMATION

MAJOR TEACHING AREAS:															
YEAR															
RANK															
POINT SCORE															
SUBJECT AREA															

ELIGIBILITY LIST INFORMATION

MAJOR TEACHING AREAS:															
YEAR															
RANK															
POINT SCORE															
SUBJECT AREA															

EMPLOYMENT DATA

Employment Date _____   Annual Salary _____ Level _____ Step _____

Status _____   Vice _____

School _____   Subject _____

City Resident _____ Yes _____ No   Increment Date _____

	Yes	No		Yes	No
Teaching Certificate Verified	☐	☐	Physical Examination	☐	☐
Degree Verified	☐	☐	Negative X-Ray or TB Test	☐	☐
Transcript Received	☐	☐			
Loyalty Oath Taken	☐	☐			
Social Security Number Verified	☐	☐			
Proof of Age Submitted	☐	☐			
Payroll Forms Completed	☐	☐			

 THE CARNEGIE

APPLICATION FOR EMPLOYMENT
4400 Forbes Avenue. Pittsburgh. PA 15213-4080

An Equal Opportunity Employer
Federal, State and local laws prohibit discrimination because of race, color, sex, age,
religion, creed, national origin, ancestry or non job-related handicap or disability.

Social Security No. _____ Date _____

Legal Name _____ Telephone _____
      (last)   (first)   (middle)

If your former employment, references, education or military service are under a name other than indicated above, please state such name.

_____
      (last)   (first)   (middle)

Present Address _____ How Long at
      (street)   (city)   (state)   (zip)   This Address _____

Previous Address _____
      (street)   (city)   (state)   (zip)

Are you at least 18 years of age? Yes _____ No _____ If you are **under** 18 list your birthdate _____

Position applied for: First Choice _____ Second Choice _____
Check which of the following you would be willing and able to work:
Full Time ☐   Part time ☐   Temporary ☐   Rotate shifts ☐
Evenings ☐   Nights ☐   Weekends ☐

State any hours and/or days that you are **not** available to work _____

On what date are you available for work? _____

Have you previously made application for employment with us? _____ If so, when? _____

Were you previously employed by us? _____ If so, when? _____ In what position? _____

EDUCATION AND TRAINING

Formal training, education or degrees which you have earned:

Names and complete address of schools or institutions	Number of years attended	Principal courses of study	Did you graduate? Degree?

Honors received, volunteer or community service or other qualifications you have which you feel are related to the position for which you are applying:

_____

WORK HISTORY

Previous work experience: Give a complete record of all employment. Start with the most recent employment

Employer's name, address and telephone number: _____

From _____ To _____ Position held _____ Last salary _____

Duties _____

_____

Name of supervisor _____ Reason for leaving _____

Employer's name, address and telephone number: _____

From _____ To _____ Position held _____ Last salary _____

Duties _____

_____

_____

Name of supervisor _____ Reason for leaving _____

Employer's name, address and telephone number: _____

From _____ To _____ Position held _____ Last salary _____

Duties _____

_____

_____

Name of supervisor _____ Reason for leaving _____

Are you legally allowed to work in the United States?   Yes _____ No _____

Have you ever served in the U.S. Armed Forces? _____ If so, which branch? _____

Have you ever pleaded guilty to, or been convicted of, a crime other than a misdemeanor or summary offense?   Yes _____ No _____

If yes, describe in full _____

— —

PLEASE READ CAREFULLY BEFORE SIGNING

I hereby certify that the foregoing statements are true and correct to the best of my knowledge and belief, and hereby grant The Carnegie permission to verify such statements and investigate all references. I understand that any false statements on this application may be considered sufficient cause for rejection of this application or for dismissal if such false information is discovered subsequent to my employment. I authorize the employers, schools and persons named above to give any information regarding my previous employment, character, general reputation and personal characteristics, together with any information they have regarding me whether or not it is in their records. I understand that, as a part of The Carnegie's procedure for processing employment applications, an investigation and/or a report may be made by a consumer reporting agency, in the process of which information may be obtained through interviews with third parties, such as family members, business associates, financial sources, friends, neighbors, or others with whom I have been acquainted. This inquiry may include information as to my character, general reputation, personal characteristics, and mode of living, whichever may be applicable. I hereby authorize The Carnegie to conduct such an investigation and/or have such a report made. I understand that under the Federal Fair Credit Reporting Act, I have the right to make a written request within a reasonable period of time for a complete and accurate disclosure by The Carnegie of the nature and scope of any investigation requested by it of a consumer reporting agency. If my application for employment is denied either wholly or partly because of information contained in a consumer report from a consumer reporting agency, I understand that The Carnegie shall so advise me, and shall supply the name and address of the consumer reporting agency making the report. I hereby release said agency, The Carnegie, my prior employers, schools, other organizations and persons from all liability for any damage for issuing this information. In addition, if accepted for employment, I hereby agree to abide by the rules and regulations of The Carnegie, and I understand that the location of my work assignment and my work shift may be changed as necessary. Further, I understand that my employment can be terminated at any time at the option of either The Carnegie or myself. I also understand that any modification of this arrangement must be reduced to writing and signed by me and an authorized representative of The Carnegie.

Signed: _____   Date: _____

Revised 6/92

APPENDIX C
PROFESSIONAL LIBRARY ASSOCIATIONS

Name: American Library Association

Mission: "To provide leadership for the development, promotion, and improvement of library and information services and the profession of librarianship in order to enhance learning and ensure access to information for all."

Members: State, public, school, and academic libraries; special libraries serving persons in government, commerce and industry, the arts, the armed services, hospitals, prisons, and other institutions and include librarians, library trustees, and other interested persons from every state and many countries of the world.

Officers (change each year): President, president-elect, treasurer. An executive board is elected by the council and the council is elected by the membership.

What you may expect for your membership: Eleven issues of *American Libraries*, discounts on ALA publications and graphics, member rates at ALA conferences, voting and committee privileges, insurance privileges, eligibility to join round tables and divisions and a copy of the *ALA Handbook of Organization* (upon request).

DIVISIONS OF THE AMERICAN LIBRARY ASSOCIATION

Name: American Association of School Librarians

Mission: To improve and extend library media services in elementary and secondary schools as a means of strengthening the overall educational program. A division of ALA, AASL holds areas of mutual concern, i.e., to represent and interpret the need for the function of school libraries to other educational and lay groups, to stimulate professional growth, and to improve the status of school librarians.

Members: A total of 7,078 members serve on 64 separate committees.

Officers: Include the executive committee comprised of president, president-elect, past president, secretary, treasurer, regional directors, and committee facilitator.

161

Conferences: This association holds its conference(s) in conjunction with the American Library Association. AASL's next national conference (with exhibits) is scheduled for Portland, Oregon.

What you may expect for your membership: Subscriptions to *School Library Media Quarterly* and *AASL Presidential Hotline*/"Connections."

Name: Association for College and Research Libraries

Mission: To foster the profession of academic and research librarianship and to enhance the ability of academic and research libraries to serve effectively the library and information needs of current and potential library users. The major goals of the organization are 1) to contribute to the total professional development of academic and research librarians; 2) to improve service capabilities of academic and research librarians; 3) to promote and speak for the interests of academic and research librarianship; and 4) to promote study and research relevant to academic and research librarianship.

Members: Total 9,496 personal members in college and research libraries, including community college libraries and 1,143 organization members.

Officers: Elected annually.

Conferences: Held in conjunction with ALA. Also individual conferences are held every two years. Each state also has an ACRL chapter.

What you may expect for your membership: One-year subscription to 6 bi-monthly journal issues of *College & Research Libraries* and 11 issues of *College & Research Libraries News*.

Name: Association for Library Collections and Technical Services

Mission: Acquisition, identification, cataloging, classification, and preservation of library materials; the development and coordination of the country's library resources; and those areas of selection and evaluation involved in the acquisition of library materials and pertinent to the development of library resources. Specifically, the ALCTS is responsible for the following tasks: research and review of the above activities; the manner in which the projects are carried out; synthesis of activities of all units within ALA that have an effect on the assigned activities; the manner of representation and interpretation of relations with groups outside the profession; stimulation of development of librarians involved, and the participation of members in various division, which are related; and planning the development of programs for research for the type of activity for the entire profession.

Members: Basically from all libraries, academic, public, and research because this association deals with the technical service aspect of the library.

Officers: Elected annually; conferences are held annually with ALA.

What you may expect for your membership: One receives *Library Resources and Technical Services* (quarterly journal) and *ALCTS Newsletter* (8 issues per year. The *Newsletter on Serials Pricing Issues* is available through ALANET, Bitnet, Datalink, and EBSCONET.

Name: Association for Library Services to Children

Mission: "The improvement and extension of library services to children in all types of libraries." ALSC is responsible for the evaluation and selection of book and nonbook library materials and for the improvement of techniques of library service to children from preschool through the eighth grade or junior high school age, when such materials and techniques are intended for use in more than one type of library.

Members: Trustees and associate members, foreign librarians, student members, honorary members, life members, continuing members, and other special members.

Officers: President, a president-elect, an executive director, and a treasurer.

Conferences: This association meets at the same time as ALA.

What you may expect for your membership: *Journal of Youth Services in Libraries* (quarterly), and *ALSC Newsletter* (semi-annual).

Name: Association of Specialized and Cooperative Library Agencies

Mission: 1) Development and evaluation of goals and plans for state library agencies, specialized library agencies, and multitype library cooperatives to facilitate the implementation, improvement, and extension of library activities designed to foster improved user services, coordinating such activities with other appropriate ALA units; 2) representation and interpretation of the role, functions, and services of state library agencies, specialized library agencies, and multitype library cooperatives within and outside the profession; 3) establishment, evaluation, and promotion of standards and service guidelines relating to the concerns of this association.

Members: Include any state or provincial library agency, specialized library agency, unit within organizations providing specialized library services, multitype library cooperative organization or agency, or any person related to or interested in such organizations or agencies, by becoming a member of ALA and selecting divisional membership in this association.

Officers: President, vice-president; elected annually.

Conferences: Held in conjunction with ALA.

What you may expect for your membership: *Interface* (quarterly).

Name: Library Administration and Management Association

Mission: To provide an organizational framework for encouraging the study of administrative theory, for improving the practice of administration in libraries, and for identifying and fostering administrative skill.

Members: All types of librarians are encouraged to apply for membership as well as affiliated groups, i.e., teachers, publishers, and non-profit organizations. Yearly membership does bear a direct relationship with the annual budget of the organization seeking membership.

Officers: Elected for a one-year term and attend an orientation session during the association's annual conference.

Conferences: Held in conjunction with ALA.

What you may expect for your membership: Members receive the LAMA quarterly journal which has a subscription price of $45 a year for nonmembers.

Name: Public Library Association (PLA)

Mission: To advance the development and effectiveness of public library service and public librarians.
      The following are objectives to achieve the mission: 1) to raise the awareness of public librarians about the issues related to free and equal access to information; 2) to develop a coordinated program for continuing education, which includes conference programming, preconferences, regional workshops, and publications; 3) to provide a public library information service for inquiries on public library issues; 4) to initiate, support, and disseminate information on new research projects on public library service or management; 5) to develop and implement public relations on the national level to increase awareness of the diverse nature and value of public library services; 6) to provide public libraries with planning and evaluation tools and to advocate and encourage the utilization of these tools; 7) to ensure that ALA and other units within ALA keep literacy a high priority; 8) to develop a strategic plan to address public library funding issues; and 9) to develop a plan to assist PLA in addressing member interests regarding distinct constituencies by the public library.

Members: Public librarians, however, any member of ALA may join PLA.

Officers: President, vice-president (president-elect), past president, and a six-member board of directors. Each section of PLA also has a board of directors. All officers serve a term of one year.

Conferences: Meets in conjunction with ALA. Also there will be two Chicago Cluster Workshops; and the Sixth National Conference will be held in Portland.

What you may expect for your membership: Members receive *Public Libraries* (a quarterly journal) and occasionally, *Public Library Reporter*.

Name: Reference and Adult Service Division

Mission: To stimulate and support in every type of library the delivery of reference/information services to all groups, regardless of age, and of general library services to adults. Began in the 1950s as two separate divisions, the Reference Division and the Adult Services Division which joined in 1970s.

Members: Include over 5,000 members, mostly public services librarians. The Division itself contains four different sub-sections: Business Reference and Services Section, Collection Development and Evaluation Section, History Section, and Machine Assisted Reference Section.

Officers: President and vice-president elected for one-year terms

Conferences: Held in conjunction with ALA

What you may expect for your membership: *RQ* (quarterly) and the *RASD Newsletter*

Name: American Society of Information Science

Mission: Bridges the gap between all information professionals, promotes professional growth, and keeps members abreast of what is happening in a rapidly changing field.

Members: Open to those in any area of the information science profession and within the organization; there are many special interest groups.

Officers: President, secretary, and treasurer (one year terms) and an eight-member executive board.

Conferences: Annual and mid-year conferences.

What you may expect for your membership: Subscriptions to *Bulletin* and *Journal of the American Society for Information Science*, career services such as the ASIS Placement Center and Jobline (a monthly listing of career positions available in all fields of information, free membership in a special interest group, discounted registration at ASIS meetings, discounts on books and monographs, and discounts on insurance, travel, and various other publications).

ASIS SIGs were created in 1966 as the professional/technical branches of ASIS. They provide members with similar professional specialties the opportunity to exchange ideas and keep themselves informed about current and discrete developments in their fields. The 21 SIGs represent various aspects of computer science, mathematics, engineering, librarianship, chemistry, linguistics, and education such as library automation networks (LAN), medical information systems (MED), and technology, information, and society (TIS).

Name: Special Library Association (SLA)

Mission: A not-for-profit, international organization serving librarians in business, governmental, museum, and "specialized departments" in larger libraries.

Members: 12,000 in 27 divisions and 55 chapters

Officers: President, president-elect, past president, secretary, chair and chair-elect of the chapter cabinet, chair and chair-elect of the division cabinet, all one-year terms.

Conferences: The annual one-week conference is usually held in June. A brief two-day winter grouping of SLA members is held in January.

To become an active member, contact the association's office at 1700 18th Street NW, Washington, DC.

OTHER NATIONAL ASSOCIATIONS

**Name: Association for Educational Communications
and Technology (AECT)**

Mission: The improvement of instruction through the utilization of media and technology and to provide leadership in educational communications and technology by linking technology and its application to the learning process.

Members: Library and microcomputer specialists, education administrators, researchers, teachers and professors, media service directors, learning resource specialists, curriculum developers, television producers and directors, and a variety of other professionals.

Officers: President, president-elect, (one-year terms), and secretary-treasurer (three year term).

Conferences: Held yearly.

What you may expect for your membership: Subscription to *Tech Trends*, free newsletters and membership directory, a discounted subscription rate for *Educational Technology Research and Development* (AECT's quarterly journal), significant discounts on non-periodical publications in the field of educational technology, low rates on insurance, information on employment opportunities, and special discounts on products.

Divisions of AECT:
(all conferences held in conjunction with AECT)

How to become an active member of any division of AECT: Join AECT. One division is free and each additional division is $10.

Name: Division of Educational Media Management

Mission: Creates guidelines on educational media management and sponsors programs to enhance media management skills.

Members: Media specialists, librarians, curriculum specialists, administrators, and educators.

Officers: President-elect, president, past-president, and board of directors (one year terms).

Name: Division of Interactive Systems and Computers

Mission: To link professionals holding a common interest in the generation, access, organization, storage and delivery of all forms of information used in the process of education and training.

Members: Librarians, teachers, television producers, media service directors, college professors, and computer specialists.

How to become an active member: Complete AECT membership form and choose DISC membership.

What you may expect for your membership: DISC members receive a bimonthly newsletter and AECT report.

Name: Division of School Media Specialists

Mission: Promotes communication among school media personnel who share a common concern in the development, implementation, and evaluation of school media programs; and strives to increase learning and improve instruction in the school setting through the utilization of educational media and technology.

Members: Library media specialists in schools, college professors, a training director of a military organization, and a media specialist from a commercial organization.

Name: Division of Instructional Development

Mission: To study, evaluate, and refine design processes; create new models of instructional development; disseminate findings; and promote academic programs.

Members: Primarily school librarians, students, professors, and audiovisual directors.

Officers: President, president-elect, past president.

Name: International Division

Mission: To improve international communication among those involved in educational technology, as well as to promote research and applied technology to support international social and economic development.

Members: School librarians and audiovisual and television production personnel.

Officers: President, president-elect, and past president.

Name: American Association of Law Librarians

Mission: Keep members of the 29 local chapters of the organization aware of new information in the areas of legal, history, and law books, information services for the public, online bibliographic services, international law, government documents, contemporary social problems, automation development, state and local law libraries, and the education of law librarians. The association also encourages new research in any area relating to law libraries.

Members: Librarians who serve the legal profession in courts, bar associations, law societies, law school, private law firms, federal, state, and county governments.

Officers: President, vice-president/president-elect, secretary, treasurer, and immediate past president (one year terms)

Conferences: Annual conference.

How to become an active member: Join national and regional separately.

What you may expect for your membership: Monthly newsletter and the quarterly *Law Library Journal.*

Name: Medical Library Association

Mission: Fostering of medical and allied scientific libraries and the exchange of medical literature of its members.

Members: 58,000 medical and allied health science library professionals.

Officers: President, executive secretary, five-member executive council (one year terms).

Conferences: Annual conferences.

How to become an active member: Find a local chapter and inquire, or contact Medical Library Association, 6 N. Michigan Avenue Suite 300, Chicago, IL 60602 (312-419-9094).

What you may expect for your membership: Opportunities to expand one's knowledge through seminars, workshops, and publications; subscription to *Bulletin*, annual *Directory*, periodic reports on medical serials, annual updates on *Medical Reference Works (1679-1966)*, recruitment brochures and video materials.

Name: Music Library Association

Mission: To promote the establishment, growth, and use of music libraries; to encourage the collection of music and musical literature in libraries; to further studies in music bibliography; and to increase the effectiveness of music library services.

Officers: President (two years), president-elect, past-president, recording secretary, treasurer, and executive secretary (one year).

Conferences: Annual conferences held each spring. Conferences include roundtables, sessions, networking, placement tables for job hunters, usually a concert, and walking and bus tours of the city's music libraries.

How to become an active member: Send name, address, and institution to Business Office, MLA, Inc., P.O. Box 487, Canton, MA 02021.

What you may expect for your membership: Individual members are entitled to vote on the business of the MLA and are encouraged to participate actively in ongoing projects and committee work. MLA publications include a monthly edition of *Music Cataloging Bulletin*, a quarterly *MLA Newsletter*, and job placement information.

Name: Society of American Archivists

Mission: This is the national professional association of "individuals and institutions concerned with the identification, preservation, and use of records of historic value."

Members: "Drawn from governments, colleges and universities, historical societies, museums, libraries, businesses, and religious institutions."

Officers: President, vice-president, treasurer and council members.

Conferences: Annual.

What you may expect for your membership: Quarterly *American Archivist*; newsletter published six times a year; member rates on annual meeting registration and publications; job placement service; opportunity to participate in sections and roundtables.

INTERNATIONAL ASSOCIATIONS

Name: International Association of School Librarianship

Mission: Encourage development of school libraries and library programs, promote professional preparation for school librarians, foster collaboration between members including literature loans and exchanges, encourage development of school library materials, and initiate and coordinate activities, conferences, and projects in school libraries.

Members: Individuals engaged in library service; school superintendents; school libraries, both primary and secondary; educational institutions related to school library services; and organizations.

Officers: President, vice-president, treasurer, executive secretary, and board of directors (for three year terms, with a two-term limit).

Conferences: Annual conferences. Conferences are held in countries all around the world.

How to become an active member: Send an application form along with payment of dues to the International Association of School Librarianship Secretariat, P.O. Box 1486, Kalamazoo, MI 49005.

What you may expect for your membership: *IASL Newsletter* and reduced registration fees for the annual conference.

Name: International Federation of Library Associations and Institutions

Members: Librarians, associations, and institutions from countries all over the world.

Officers: President (four years) and coordinating board.

Conferences: Annual conferences.

ANNOTATED BIBLIOGRAPHY

GENERAL REFERENCES FOR
LIBRARY MANAGEMENT

Drucker, Peter F. *Managing the Non-Profit Organization: Principles and Practices.* New York: HarperCollins, 1990.

Drucker presents five parts: "The Mission Comes First: And Your Role As a Leader," with one intriguing chapter titled "Leadership Is a Foul-Weather Job"; "From Mission to Performance: Effective Strategies for Marketing, Innovation, and Fund Development"; "Managing for Performance: How to Define It; How to Measure It"; "People and Relationships: Your Staff, Your Board, Your Volunteers, Your Community"; and "Developing Yourself: As a Person, As an Executive, As a Leader."

Harrison, Colin, and Rosemary Beenham. *The Basics of Librarianship.* 2d ed. London: Clive Bingley, 1980.

This title and that by St. Clair and Williamson are basic management guides. Because they are published in Great Britain, they have an English flavor and examples are given for libraries in the Commonwealth, where book cards become "transaction" cards.

Reed, Sally Gardner. *Small Libraries: A Handbook for Successful Management.* Jefferson, N.C.: McFarland, [1990].

"The purpose of this book is to share ways to give your library a place of strength in the community. Creating a solid base of political support, offering top-notch service to everyone in the community no matter how diverse their needs or how small their number, maintaining a useful and used collection, developing and nurturing a competent and productive staff. . . . The result will be exceptional library service for those in even the statistically smallest of communities" (preface).

St. Clair, Guy, and Joan Williamson. *Managing the One-Person Library.* London: Butterworths, 1986.

One foreword is written by the executive director of the Special Libraries Association, indicating that the book is directed to libraries in organizations or smaller libraries in academic institutions. However, the chapter on "Professional Isolation and Independence" gives excellent suggestions for overcoming isolation while "enhancing the benefits of independence."

CHAPTER 1: YOUR LIBRARY

Policies, Forms, Budgeting as Management

Adams, Helen R. *School Media Policy Development: A Practical Process for Small Districts*. Littleton, Colo.: Libraries Unlimited, 1986. 174pp.

This multipurpose volume includes an argument for developing policies; beginning the process; working with outside consultants, staff, students, and the community; working with the administration and the board of education; and making policies work. A case study weaves the theory into practice. The appendixes include case study district policies as well as job descriptions and performance evaluations for the district library media director, the media specialist, the audiovisual director, and the high school adult media center aide.

Cassell, Kay Ann, and Elizabeth Futas. *Developing Library Collections, Policies, and Procedures: A How-to-Do-It Manual for Small and Medium-Sized Libraries*. How-to-Do-It Manuals for Libraries, no. 12. New York: Neal-Schuman, 1991. 143pp.

The authors describe this as a manual for creating collection development policies that will help librarians plan their collections. Described are how to set goals, objectives, and priorities; how to learn about the current collection in relationship to the community; and how to develop evaluation procedures to test new policies.

Dewey, Barbara I. *Raising Money for Academic and Research Libraries*. How-to-Do-It Manuals for Libraries, no. 18. New York: Neal-Schuman, 1991. 138pp.

Although this title is intended for the academic librarian, topics are addressed that will be helpful for a librarian in a smaller library. For instance, the basic steps in the planning process are applicable to any library, as is the chapter on establishing friends groups for fund-raising.

Futas, Elizabeth. *The Library Forms Illustrated Handbook*. New York: Neal-Schuman, 1984. 875pp.

The author states that the book's objective is "to share the forms in libraries around the country with all the profession." Based on actual library forms, the book includes "Technical Services"—acquisition, cataloging, and circulation forms; "Public Services"—reference, online searching, interlibrary loan, and bibliographic instruction forms; "Administrative Services"—personnel, nonpersonnel, and budget forms; "Audiovisual Services"—software, hardware, and statistics forms; and "Special Collections"—oral history, public library, and academic library forms.

Gervasi, Anne, and Betty Kay Seibt. *Handbook for Small, Rural, and Emerging Public Libraries*. Phoenix, Ariz.: Oryx Press, 1988. 196pp.

"This book . . . is about providing library services to areas that are not part of large metropolitan centers and to areas that have not had library service before. This is also a book for the managers of existing libraries who are feeling the need to upgrade or alter services, or revitalize the library's place in the community" (p. 3). Included are getting started, options for service, analyzing the community, legal issues, publicity and fund-raising, facilities, choosing the library director, selection policies, building the collection, technical processes, circulation, reference and reader's advisory, programming, management, furnishing the library, and cooperative services. The appendixes include a community survey form, state library addresses, and telephone numbers with some of their services. Brief forms for reconsideration of library materials, donations, video loan user agreement, programming record, task assignments, and a volunteer record are also reproduced in an appendix.

Ihrig, Alice B. *Decision-Making for Public Libraries*. Hamden, Conn.: Library Professional Publications, 1989. 166pp.

The author attempts to help develop decision-making skills by presenting information on the structure and scope of public library boards, the criteria for selection of library trustees, and the relationship between library trustees and the director. Carefully detailed are the types of decisions, the bases for decision making, procedures for making better decisions, and the influence of trustees on decision making.

Jacob, M. E. L. *Strategic Planning: A How-to-Do-It Manual for Libraries*. How-to-Do-It Manuals for Libraries, no. 9. New York: Neal-Schuman, 1990. 120pp.

The author encourages readers to duplicate the forms included and use them in creating a planning workbook. The author suggests: "Strategic planning focuses on the vision of what a library or institution desires to be: Where a library is going, how it will get there, which obstacles it should avoid, and how it can effectively meet its community's needs." Guidelines are given for those who should fully participate in the strategic planning process. Special attention is given to resource allocation for developing the plan, which includes checklists for each step of the process.

Karpisek, Marian. *Policymaking for School Library Media Programs*. Chicago: American Library Association, 1989. 164pp.

The author describes the eight steps of policy writing: research, first draft, committee consideration, final draft, committee review, administrative approval, faculty and parent dissemination, and student awareness. The library media philosophy is discussed. Circulation, scheduling, selection, book ordering and budgeting, accounting and materials processing, inventory and weeding, and paraprofessionals and volunteers are presented. As is stated in the preface, this books extends "beyond the definition of philosophy and policy" and "provides a framework of management procedures by which the library media specialist enacts policy into practice."

Lindsey, Jonathan A., and Ann E. Prentice. *Professional Ethics and Librarians*. Phoenix, Ariz.: Oryx Press, 1985. 103pp.

From the foreword: "In a technological age in which the volume of information generated increases exponentially, the librarian has been forced to pick and choose more carefully and, reluctantly, to charge users for services that go beyond the basic level. The more money changes hands, the more the client comes to rely on the information provided, the greater the consequences will be for the librarian who provides wrong or inaccurate information." This volume discusses developing an ethics code, reproduces American Library Codes of Ethics, and shares commentary on the code by nine librarians.

Riggs, Donald E. *Strategic Planning for Library Managers*. Phoenix, Ariz.: Oryx Press, 1984. 137pp.

Strategic planning is described as defining the terms, organizing participants, identifying policies, and developing mission, goals, and objectives. Also discussed are alternatives and contingencies for when things go awry and the library program must be saved. Stating policies and planning for resource allocation are detailed. A management information system (MIS), Planning Programming Budgeting System (PPBS), and a systems approach are presented so that the reader might compare the three. The chapter on implementing strategic planning includes activity charts and a one-year planning cycle chart. Ways to evaluate and a suggested scale for evaluating the library's strategic planning system conclude the book.

Toor, Ruth, and Hilda K. Weisburg. *Complete Book of Forms for Managing the School Library*. West Nyack, N.Y.: Center for Applied Research in Education, 1982. 256pp.

The authors have prepared "a one-stop source for all of the forms [170 total] needed to manage today's media center." They include "Forms for Analyzing Your Facilities and Collection," "Forms for Developing Personnel Relationships and Organizing Clerical/Volunteer Staff," "Forms for Circulation Control," "Forms for Technical Services," "Forms for Managing Library Programs," "Forms for Working with Teachers," "Forms for Working with Administration," "Forms for Correspondence," "Forms for End-of-Year Activities," and "Forms for Professional Growth and Development." Although forms are targeted for the school library, most can be used in other types of libraries.

Vertical Files

Sitter, Clare. *The Vertical File and Its Alternatives: A Handbook*. Englewood, Colo.: Libraries Unlimited, 1992. 275pp.

Based on a previous book, *The Vertical File and Its Satellites*, 2d ed. (Libraries Unlimited, 1979) by Shirley Miller, this reference is a step-by-step guide to working with vertical files. The author suggests ways to find resources and how to label, file, weed, and circulate materials. Also covered are organizing and preserving pamphlets and clippings and how to promote special collections of these materials. A glossary and list of vendors are included.

Technologies

Buckland, Michael. *Information and Information Systems*. New York: Greenwood, 1991. 225pp.

Because the print is small, this appears to be a highly technical book. However, it has many definitions and presents concepts in a way beginners can understand. The author's intention was to "provide a general introduction to information systems, their nature, and how they relate to their contexts." Chapter 7 highlights "Information Technology" and discusses this in the process of handling information. This will be helpful to any manager of a library.

Costa, Betty, and Marie Costa. *A Micro Handbook for Small Libraries and Media Centers*. 3d ed. Englewood, Colo.: Libraries Unlimited, 1991. 325pp.

This newly revised edition covers the newest hardware and software for library applications. The practical explanations and recent references to sources will help even those with little knowledge of computers and their applications. Bibliographies at the end of each chapter introduce additional information. Of particular interest may be the information related to CD-ROMs, electronic bulletin boards, and managing local area networks.

CHAPTER 2: USERS IN THE LIBRARY

Public Relations

Laughlin, Mildred Knight, and Kathy Howard Latrobe. *Public Relations for School Library Media Centers*. Englewood, Colo.: Libraries Unlimited, 1990. 133pp.

Written by the authors and 14 others including faculty members, school library media specialists, and a state department of education consultant this book covers developing a public relations plan, meeting the needs of special clienteles, positive student behavior management, as well as working with parents and the community, the public library, and the media, and developing a public relations presentation. One chapter covers "outside the community," including lobbying legislators. The final chapter discusses evaluating the success of your PR program.

Roberts, Anne F., and Susan Griswold Blandy. *Public Relations for Librarians*. Englewood, Colo.: Libraries Unlimited, 1989. 184pp.

This book is divided into three parts: "Setting the Scene," "Practicing the Art," and "Finding the Help." Graphics, forms, and many examples enhance this text, which also has good bibliographies of suggested readings. Included is an evaluative bibliography of books directly related to public relations such as *Clip Art & Dynamic Designs for Libraries & Media Centers*.

Tuggle, Ann Montgomery, and Dawn Hansen Heller. *Grand Schemes and Nitty-Gritty Details: Library PR That Works*. Littleton, Colo.: Libraries Unlimited, 1987. 237pp.

Drawings and photographs illustrate public relations ideas gathered from a wide geographic area and including all types of libraries. The section "Nitty-Gritty Details" includes "How to Design and Judge Public Relations Programs: A Planned Approach," "How to Communicate 'Live': Mastering Public Speaking," "How to Communicate in Print: Write, Write—Right!," and "How to Communicate with Images: Seeing Is Believing."

Facilities

Anderson, Pauline H. *Planning School Library Media Facilities*. Hamden, Conn.: Library Professional Publications, 1990. 260pp.

This book discusses the politics of preplanning, planning, developing the planning process, design, construction, and the move into the new facility. The author has collected examples from librarians who have recently built new facilities and who have shared their planning processes. The "Cardinal Guidelines," suggested phases, space allocations, and spacial relationships described will be helpful to anyone planning a new facility.

Boss, Richard W. *Information Technologies and Space Planning and Libraries and Information Centers*. Boston: G. K. Hall, 1987. 121pp.

"Dramatic changes in information technologies have occurred in the past two decades, especially in the use of library automation and digital telefacsimile," Boss states. He describes the information technologies available and provides usage, housing, and placement in the facility suggestions.

Fraley, Ruth A., and Carol Lee Anderson. *Library Space Planning: A How-to-Do-It Manual for Allocating and Reorganizing Collections, Resources, and Facilities*. How-to-Do-It Manuals for Libraries, no. 5. New York: Neal-Schuman, 1990. 194pp.

The authors discuss how to prepare a space plan based on goals and objectives written after analyzing reasons for space reorganization. Guidelines for measuring the collection are given, with alternatives for collection-space dilemmas, such as compact shelving, converting the collection to microform, and off-site storage. A chapter on assessing facilities, furniture, and equipment includes weight-loading walls and columns and pillars. Also included are chapters on budgeting, publicity, how to select a way to accomplish the move, how to continue operations during the move, and the actual move. Appendixes include bid specifications and a sample bid.

Klasing, Jane P. *Designing and Renovating School Library Media Centers*. Chicago: American Library Association, 1991. 114pp.

Stressing the school planning team, this volume provides a model for writing educational specifications, discusses renovation, and provides a case study for new construction. The glossary and the explanation of architectural symbols are especially helpful. Another useful appendix is the sample "Invitation to Bid."

Lushington, Nolan, and James M. Kusack. *The Design and Evaluation of Public Library Buildings*. Hamden, Conn.: Library Professional Publications, 1991. 250pp.

Contents include library design and user experience, planning library buildings, and building on an existing facility. This is a well illustrated, practical approach to building or renovating a library.

CHAPTER 3: STAFFING IN THE LIBRARY

Personnel

Giesecke, Joan, ed. *Practical Help for New Supervisors*. Chicago: American Library Association, 1992. 69pp.

This book was prepared by the Supervisory Skills Committee, the Library Personnel Section of the Library Administration and Management Association, a division of the American Library Association. Covered are "Interviewing," "Orienting the New Library Employee," "Performance Appraisal," "Rewarding Employees Nonmonetarily," "Communication," "Managing Change," and "Effective Meetings." Bibliographies at the end of chapters include citations to periodical articles, as well as books and chapters in books.

Lipow, Ann Grodzins, and Deborah A. Carver, eds. *Staff Development: A Practical Guide*. 2d ed. Chicago: American Library Association, 1992. 102pp.

Prepared by the Staff Development Committee, Personnel Administration Section of the Library Administration and Management Association, a division of the American Library Association, this guide includes two parts. The first is "to give the reader a theoretical background to many of the chapters which appear in the second section." The second is a reference for the person planning or designing the staff development program and includes "How to Pay for Programs," "How to Find Expert Speakers or Presenters," "How to Prepare for a Specific Program," "How to Make an Effective Presentation," "How to Evaluate Your Program," and "How to Develop Training Skills."

Plate, Kenneth H. *Library Manager's Workbook: Problem-Solving in the Supervision of Information Service Personnel*. Studio City, Calif.: Pacific Information, 1985. 101pp.

The author states that this volume is the result of "many workshops involving hundreds of library supervisors." It covers "The Supervisor-Employee Relationship," "The Supervisor-Superior Relationship," "The Supervisor and Lateral Relationships," "Situational Analysis: Basic Tools," and "Job Design and Performance Evaluation." The final chapter includes common problems of supervisory applications, such as collective agreements and employee productivity, among others.

Volunteers

Bennett, Linda Leveque. *Volunteers in the School Media Center*. Littleton, Colo.: Libraries Unlimited, 1984. 236pp.

The author analyzes the impact of a volunteer program on budget, services, staff, and the volunteers. Discussion of apprehensions includes job insecurity, problem masking, lack of control, exploitation, and costs. Also covered are preplanning, choosing a coordinator, and attracting and screening volunteers. Finally, placing volunteers, training and implementation, anticipating and correcting problems, recognizing assistance, and evaluating and modifying the volunteer program are discussed. Appendixes include guidelines, sample evaluations, and sample manuals.

Karp, Rashelle S. *Volunteers in Libraries.* Small Libraries Publication, no. 20. Chicago: Library Administration and Management Association, 1993. 10pp.

This short publication describes the way to a successful volunteer program through planning, recruiting, making the decision to hire, orientation and training, evaluation, and recognition. A chart lists the volunteer's rights and responsibilities. "Where to Get Help" suggests placing the library address on the mailing lists of seven agencies whose primary activities are in volunteerism.

Management

Dutton, Sue. *The Effective Trustee Handbook.* Ottawa: Canadian Library Association, 1987.

This is a simple, step-by-step presentation of board management including chairing meetings, setting agendas, paying attention to parliamentary procedures, and resource management including planning, policies and procedures, and financial information.

Young, Virginia G., ed. *The Library Trustee: A Practical Guidebook.* 4th ed. Chicago: American Library Association, 1988. 230pp.

This is a compilation of articles by authorities in the field of public libraries and their trustees. Chapters include "Organization of the Library Board," "The Trustee as Policymaker," "Trustee Relationships with Librarian and Staff," "The Trustee and the Law," "The Trustee as Advocate," "The Trustee and the State Library," and "The Trustee and Intellectual Freedom." Appendixes offer a trustee orientation program, guidelines for a library policy, a sample book selection policy, a sample public relations policy, an ethics statement for public library trustees, an indemnification statement, a budget checklist, sample by-laws, evaluation of the library director, evaluation of board members, rules for volunteers, and forming a Friends group.

CHAPTER 4: CIRCULATION OF MATERIALS AND EQUIPMENT

Copyright

Strong, William S. *The Copyright Book: A Practical Guide.* 3d ed. Cambridge, Mass.: MIT Press, 1990. 249pp.

A concise book presenting "The Subject Matter of Copyright," "Ownership," "Transfers of Copyright," "Copyright Notice," "Registration of a Copyright Claim," "Rights in Copyrighted Works," "The Compulsory Licenses," "Infringement and Fair Use," "Works Created Before 1978," "Tax Treatment of Copyrights," and "International Copyright Protection." This book will serve as a reference for library users who ask questions about copyright as well as for accidental librarians who need to confirm copyright regulations for themselves.

CHAPTER 5: REFERENCE IN THE LIBRARY

Bopp, Richard E., and Linda C. Smith. *Reference and Information Services: An Introduction.* 2d ed. Englewood, Colo.: Libraries Unlimited, 1995. 626pp.

An overview of the most important tools for general reference and the concepts and theory behind reference services. The first half covers theory and concepts, including philosophy of reference service, the reference interview, principles and goals of library instruction, and bibliographic control. Training and continuing education for reference staff, evaluation of reference services, and management of services complete the first part. The remainder of the book discusses characteristics of particular types of reference books.

Hillyard, James M. *Where to Find What: A Handbook to Reference Service,* revised and updated ed. Metuchen, N.J.: Scarecrow Press, 1984. 357pp.

This author has taken 595 subject headings and located books that have references to these subject headings. If you wish to find information on tennis, this author suggests the *Official Encyclopedia of Tennis* or *Office Tennis Yearbook and Guide,* and refers to either *World Almanac and Book of Facts* or *Information Please Almanac* for recent tournament winners and records.

Katz, William A. *Introduction to Reference Work.* Vol. 1. *Reference Services and Reference Processes.* Vol. 2. 6th ed. New York: McGraw-Hill, 1992.

Volume 1 has detailed descriptions of reference books used for each type of question, e.g., the chapters on dictionaries describe dictionaries and on indexes describe the most appropriate indexes to use for each subject area.

Volume 2 presents the reference interview and explains how to get the questioner to restate the question. It explains manual searches through development of a search strategy and provides information on online reference services, online searches, databases, microcomputers and CD-ROM, and bibliographic networks. It includes information on library instruction and how to evaluate reference services. Each chapter has a bibliography of suggested reading.

Katz, William A., ed. *Reference and Information Services: A Reader for the Nineties.* Metuchen, N.J.: Scarecrow Press, 1991. 415pp.

"The purpose of this collection . . . is to bring together in a single, convenient place a representative view of today's reference and information services." The author has collected articles from a variety of library periodicals written by leaders in the field, classifying them under "The Reference Process," "Ethics and Evaluation of Reference Service," "Access to Information," "Interview and Search," and "The Computer—and Beyond."

McCormick, Mona. *The New York Times Guide to Reference Materials.* Rev. ed. Popular Library Edition series. New York: Signet, 1986.

This book has five chapters: "Finding Information," "Reference Books by Type," "Reference Books in Subject Areas," "Evaluation Information," and "Organizing and Communicating Information." The paperback format makes it inexpensive to own. Examples reproduced from actual reference books point out the items of primary interest in the books cited.

Nichols, Margaret Irby. *Guide to Reference Books for School Media Centers.* 4th ed. Englewood, Colo.: Libraries Unlimited, 1992.

CHAPTER 6: SERVICES

Bloomfield, Masse. *How to Use a Library: A Guide to Literature Searching.* Canoga Park, Calif.: Masefield Books, 1991. 89pp.

This guide includes *Subject Index to Books in Print, Cumulative Book Index, Engineering Index, Psychological Abstracts, Monthly Catalog of U.S. Government Publications,* and *Government Reports Announcements and Index,* as well as computer searching on an online catalog. Also explained are standard reference tools such as encyclopedias, almanacs, yearbooks, handbooks, directories, atlases, dictionaries, and biographical aids. Published bibliographies, citation indexes, and literature guides are described.

Hede, Agnes Ann. *Reference Readiness: A Manual for Librarians and Students.* 4th ed., rev. and updated. Hamden, Conn.: Library Professional Publications, 1990. 206pp.

The authors suggest that this book will "appropriate sources" to answer "diverse questions." Each reference book is described in one or two sentences, including the arrangement of the volume. The reader is then given two to seven activities related to the reference tool that will enhance the use.

Seaver, Alice R. *Library Media Skills: Strategies for Instructing Primary Students.* 2d ed. Englewood, Colo.: Libraries Unlimited, 1991. 230pp.

Suggestions for implementing this library media skills program include planning the program, identifying the objectives and the instructional strategies, literature enrichment and awareness, evaluation, and record keeping. Part II includes units of instruction. An optional disk is available upon request.

Van Vliet, Lucille W. *Media Skills for Middle Schools: Strategies for Library Media Specialists and Teachers.* Littleton, Colo.: Libraries Unlimited, 1984. 263pp.

Part I includes "The Middle School," "The Middle School Student," "Integrated Library Media Skills," "The Role of the Library Media Specialist," and "The Role of the Teacher." Part II comprises 22 lessons and a list of resources and vendors mentioned in the text.

Zlotnick, Barbara Bradley. *Ready for Reference: Media Skills for Intermediate Students.* Littleton, Colo.: Libraries Unlimited, 1984. 274pp.

This well-illustrated volume has practical strategies and activities to help intermediate students undertake research and study skills in the library. Because it is important for teachers and librarians to work together, the activities reflect a joint effort.

CHAPTER 7: ADDING TO THE COLLECTION

Acquiring Materials

Bonk, Wallace John, and Rose Mary Magrill. *Building Library Collections*. 5th ed. Metuchen, N.J.: Scarecrow Press, 1979.

Carter, Mary Duncan, Wallace John Bonk, and Rose Mary Magrill. *Building Library Collections*. 4th ed. Metuchen, N.J.: Scarecrow Press, 1974. 415pp.
This volume is dated as far as citations to actual selection sources and documents, such as statements of the American Library Association Council. It is cited here because some librarians may have a text copy; it was often used for collection development classes in library school programs. The first and third chapters, "Principles of Selection for Public Libraries" and "Selection by Subject," remain useful, as do the chapters on "Surveying and Weeding Collections; Surveying the Community" and "Censorship and Selection." The appendixes contain sample selection policies.

Curley, Arthur, and Dorothy Broderick. *Building Library Collections*. 6th ed. Metuchen, N.J.: Scarecrow Press, 1985. 339pp.
This text covers "Why Libraries Exist," "Studying the Library's Community," "Principles of Selection for Public Libraries," "Selection Aids," "The Selector and Non-Book Materials," "Censorship and Selection," "The Publishing Trade," "Resource Sharing," "Acquisitions," "Collection Evaluation," and "Weeding, Storage, and Preservation."

Futas, Elizabeth, ed. *Library Acquisition Policies and Procedures*. 2d ed. Phoenix, Ariz.: Oryx Press, 1984. 579pp.
The value of this book is that it provides models for the librarian to build on. Policies from academic libraries and public libraries are presented. Public libraries range from larger ones such as the Cuyahoga County (Ohio) Public Library with over 100 professionals and 300 clericals to smaller ones such as the Middleton (Wisconsin) Public Library with 3 professionals and 6 clerical assistants. Partial policies are given for principles of selection, gifts, collections, clientele, limitations, networking, confidentiality, intellectual freedom, evaluation, and maintenance.

Intellectual Freedom Manual. 4th ed. Compiled by the Office for Intellectual Freedom of the American Library Association. Chicago: American Library Association, 1992. 283pp.
This work is "designed to answer the many practical questions that confront librarians in applying the principles of intellectual freedom to library service." It gives a historical overview of the association and intellectual freedom. It also presents the Library Bill of Rights and the interpretations (although these are often under review and revision), the development of the Freedom to Read statement, intellectual freedom concerns by type of library, laws governing freedom to read, essential preparations "before the censor comes," and assistance offered by the American Library Association.

Katz, William A. *Collection Development: The Selection of Materials for Libraries.* New York: Holt, Rinehart & Winston, 1980. 352pp.

This text includes "The Philosophy of Selection" with subtitles "Professionalism and Selection," "Selection and Type of Library," "Selection Objectives and Goals," "Issues in Selection Philosophy," and "Collection Development Policy Statement." "The Public and Selection" has extensive information on data gathering for a community analysis, the nonuser and the nonreader, and I&R (information and referral services). Library cooperation, formulas, and budget implications for selection are discussed. "Collection Analysis" covers "Core Literature," "Weeding," "Gifts and Exchanges," "Theft and Inventory," and "Collection Analysis and Evaluation." "Selection Process" discusses guidelines for selection, demand collections, quality, committee selection, and different library audiences. Selection of print is separated from nonprint. Print is discussed by audience, adults and children, using popular reviews, and selecting paperbacks. Ordering processes for books and periodicals are covered, and other print materials such as microforms, pamphlets, and manuscripts are discussed. A thorough coverage.

Magrill, Rose Mary, and John Corbin. *Acquisitions Management and Collection Development in Libraries.* Chicago: American Library Association, 1989. 285pp.

These authors have carried forward the task of preparing a collection development text. They discuss collection development policies and organizing collection development and acquisitions work, with less emphasis on surveying the community. They have extensive information on gifts and exchanges and evaluating the collection. The chapters "Bibliographic Searching" and "Vendor-Controlled Order Plans" will help the reader understand these processes.

Sader, Marion, ed. *Reference Books for Young Readers: Authoritative Evaluations of Encyclopedias, Atlases, and Dictionaries.* New York: R. R. Bowker, 1988. 615pp.

This excellent introduction to evaluating dictionaries, encyclopedias, and atlases includes an extensive rating of general reference books for young readers. It includes helpful illustrations of pages from encyclopedias and dictionaries pointing out such features as guide words and cross-references.

Segal, Joseph P. *Evaluating and Weeding Collections in Small and Medium-Sized Public Libraries: The CREW Method.* Chicago: American Library Association, 1980. 25pp.

This short book describes the 10-step "CREW Method" of evaluating and weeding collections. Of special interest is the discussion of "What to Do with Weeded Books: Types of Disposal."

Slote, Stanley J. *Weeding Library Collections: Library Weeding Methods.* 3d ed. Englewood, Colo.: Libraries Unlimited, 1989. 283pp.

Although this book may tell "primer" library managers more than they want to know, it does have the research on weeding as well as careful explanations of weeding practices.

Stueart, Robert D., and George B. Miller, eds. *Collection Development in Libraries: A Treatise*. Foundations in Library and Information Science Series, vol. 10. Greenwich, Conn.: Jai Press, 1980. 602pp.

This is a collection of essays by distinguished librarians and would be most useful as a reference rather than a source of daily assistance in developing collections.

Tuttle, Marcia. *Introduction to Serials Management*. Foundations in Library and Information Science Series, vol. 11. Greenwich, Conn.: Jai Press, 1983. 324pp.

This is a series of essays on serials management, the author an expert in the field, with chapters by two other experts, all at the University of North Carolina at Chapel Hill. As one might imagine, the information is slanted toward the academic librarian and would be most useful as a reference.

Van Orden, Phyllis J. *The Collection Program in Elementary and Middle Schools: Concepts, Practices, and Information Sources*. Littleton, Colo.: Libraries Unlimited, 1982. 301pp.

Although the information in this book is 13 years old, it provides "an overview of the processes and procedures associated with developing, maintaining, and evaluating a collection at the building level." From the media specialist's role through the collection, the collection program, policies, and procedures, the author discusses selection of materials with criteria by format. Meeting needs is presented in terms of the curriculum, typical individuals, and exceptional children. Administrative concerns include acquisition procedures and maintaining and evaluating the collection.

Van Orden, Phyllis J. *The Collection Program in Schools: Concepts, Practices, and Information Sources*. 2d ed. Englewood, Colo.: Libraries Unlimited, 1995. 376pp.

This is a specialized collection development book for school librarians. However, much of it can be translated for the public library. A local school librarian might have a copy to lend. Of particular interest are assessing the community, "The Collection's External Environment," "Policies and Procedures," and "Developing Policy Statements." Part II, "Selection of Materials," has selection procedures, general selection criteria, and criteria by format.

Wortman, William A. *Collection Management: Background and Principles*. Chicago: American Library Association, 1989. 243pp.

These are the author's "essays" on collection management and the format differs from the "how to do it" format of the others in this section. This would be read to assure yourself that you are functioning in the appropriate way.

Selection Tools

Because the following references are updated frequently, some of the annotations may be omitted.

Abrahamson, Richard F. *Books for You: A Booklist for Senior High Students*. 10th ed. Urbana, Ill.: National Council of Teachers of English, 1988. 507pp.

Abridged Readers' Guide to Periodical Literature. New York: H. W. Wilson, 1936—. Annual.

This volume is used to select the basic periodical collection, because unindexed periodicals are less useful. Research has shown that most patrons find their needed information in 20 of these titles. This suggests that librarians should purchase two subscriptions to the 20 most popular and share the remaining purchases with one or more other libraries.

Elementary School Library Collection: A Guide to Books and Other Media, Phases 1-2-3. 18th ed. Williamsport, PA: Brodart, 1992.

Titles in this work are recommended by a selection committee chosen by the publisher. Their aim is to meet curriculum needs and personal interests of preschool through sixth-grade students. They also suggest items to purchase for a professional collection to provide materials on child development and curriculum for teachers and administrators. Materials are in a variety of formats, including books, periodicals, filmstrips, sound recordings, kits, art and study prints, videocassettes, and microcomputer programs.

Katz, William A. *Magazines for Libraries.* 7th ed. New York: R. R. Bowker, 1992. 1212pp.

This annotated list of magazines by subject includes over 6,500 periodicals. They were carefully selected and represent what the consultants and editors thought would be the best and most useful for primary, secondary, public, academic, or special libraries. Entries are coded by level. Each annotation includes purpose, scope, audience, and usually a value judgment.

Kimmel, Margaret, and Elizabeth Segal. *For Reading Out Loud.* Rev. ed. New York: Dell, 1991. 279pp.

A list of 175 annotated titles for reading aloud to children.

Public Library Catalog. 9th ed. New York: H. W. Wilson, 1989. 1338pp.

This is a list of recommended nonfiction books for adults, classified by subject. Supplements are issued each year to bring these up-to-date until the 10th edition is compiled.

Richardson, Selma K. *Magazines for Children: A Guide for Parents, Teachers, and Librarians.* 2d ed. Chicago: American Library Association, 1991. 139pp.

Designed to help librarians who want to know about children's magazines, this book defines the curriculum subjects, activities, and exceptional qualities of different magazines. All titles listed in the first edition were reviewed to see that they "sustained their focus and quality and to note any changes in content and format" (p. vii).

Trelease, Jim. *The Read-Aloud Handbook.* 2d rev. ed. New York: Penguin Books, 1989. 290pp.

The first half presents evidence of the effects of reading aloud, including how to make this work. The last half is the "Treasury of Read-Alouds." This is a beginner's guide to recommended titles, so that busy librarians, teachers, and parents can choose books to read. All titles were in print at the time of publication.

Selecting Equipment

Equipment Directory of Video, Computer, and Audio-Visual Products. 37th ed. Fairfax, Va.: International Communications Industries Association, 1991-1992.

This annual publication contains photographs of equipment and the information needed to write specifications for each item.

Processing

Bloomberg, Marty, and G. Edward Evans. *Introduction to Technical Services for Library Technicians*. 5th ed. Littleton, Colo.: Libraries Unlimited, 1985. 397pp.

This book explains library technical services, automation and libraries, and networks, cooperatives, and automated systems for technical services; however, the accidental librarian may be most interested in the explanations of general publishing, bibliographic verification, and machine-aided verification. Lengthy descriptions are given of order procedures, accounting and bookkeeping, receipt of orders, automated acquisition, and cataloging. Finally, extensive information with illustrations is provided about descriptive cataloging, cataloging and main entry, added entry, and references. Subject headings and classification, both Library of Congress and Dewey, are covered. Order and verification procedures for serials and serials cataloging are provided. Sources of cataloging information from both bibliographic services and commercial cataloging services are given, as well as such cataloging routines as the shelf list, authority files, catalog card reproduction, filing, and statistics and reports. A glossary of terms and acronyms used in technical services is provided in the appendix.

Intner, Sheila S., and Jean Weihs. *Standard Cataloging for School and Public Libraries*. Englewood, Colo.: Libraries Unlimited, 1990. 208pp.

This is an introduction for librarians managing small libraries such as those in schools and towns. Included are chapters on "Decisions," "The *Anglo-American Cataloging Rules*," "Description," "Access," "Subject Heading Lists," "*Sears List of Subject Headings*," "*Library of Congress Subject Headings*," "Classification Systems," "The Dewey Decimal Classification," "Library of Congress Classification," "Bibliographic Utilities: Large Computer-based Networks," "Local Systems," "The MARC Formats," and "Cataloging and Classification Policies." Each chapter closes with "Recommended Reading."

Budgeting and Securing Funding

Belcher, Jane C., and Julia M. Jacobsen. *From Idea to Funded Project: Grant Proposals That Work*. 4th ed. Phoenix, Ariz.: Oryx Press, 1992.

This volume contains a list of useful resources such as acronyms, sources of assistance and training, and copies of forms and required information from actual agencies. Developing the idea through preparing the evaluation sections are included.

Trumpeter, Margo C., and Richard S. Rounds. *Basic Budgeting Practices for Librarians*. Chicago: American Library Association, 1985. 164pp.

Turock, Betty J. and Andrea Pedolsky. *Creating a Financial Plan*. How-to-Do-It Manuals for Libraries, no. 22. New York: Neal-Schuman, 1992. 188pp.
   This book is divided into "The Fundamentals," "Data Gathering," "Setting the Course," and "Staying on Course." Illustrations and worksheets help make a difficult task much easier to understand.

Woolls, Blanche. *Grant Proposal Writing: A Handbook for School Library Media Specialists*. New York: Greenwood, 1986. 131pp.
   Using one funded proposal as a model, the author discusses writing a proposal, from developing an idea and finding a funding source through submitting the completed proposal. Finally, a brief discussion covers managing a funded project.

CHAPTER 8: EVALUATING WHAT YOU DO

Information Power: Guidelines for School Library Media Programs. Chicago: American Library Association, 1988. 171pp.

Loertscher, David V. *Taxonomies of the School Library Media Program*. Englewood, Colo.: Libraries Unlimited, 1988. 336pp.

INDEX